What Makes You So Busy?

What Makes You So Busy?

Finding Peace in the Modern World

K H E N P O   S O D A R G Y E

Wisdom

Wisdom Publications
199 Elm Street
Somerville, MA 02144 USA
wisdomexperience.org

Library of Congress Cataloging-in-Publication Data
Names: Suodaji, Kanbu, 1962– author.
Title: What makes you so busy? / Khenpo Sodargye.
Description: Somerville, MA: Wisdom Publications, 2019.
Identifiers: LCCN 2019016595 (print) | ISBN 9781614295846 (pbk.: alk. paper)
Subjects: LCSH: Buddhism—Psychology. | Happiness—Religious aspects—Buddhism.
Classification: LCC BQ4570.P76 S86 2019 (print) | LCC BQ4570.P76 (ebook) |
     DDC 294.3/444—dc23
LC record available at https://lccn.loc.gov/2019016595
LC ebook record available at https://lccn.loc.gov/2019980064

ISBN 978-1-61429-584-6   ebook ISBN 978-1-61429-607-2

23 22 21 20 19
5 4 3 2 1

Translated by Ke Jiang. Cover design by Marc Whitaker. Interior design by TL. Set in Arno Pro 12/16 pt.

Contents

Preface   vii

1. Meditation and Wealth   1

2. What Is Love?   15

3. Science and the Path to Happiness   27

4. Buddhadharma in the Age of Science and Technology   43

5. Stress-Relieving Wisdom   61

6. Altruism in Buddhism   85

7. The Buddhist Low-Desire, Low-Carbon Lifestyle   101

8. Selfless Hearts Expand   113

9. Happiness Is Rooted in the Heart   129

10. How to Face Suffering   149

11. Eight Secrets to Happiness   169

12. Heart   201

Afterword   239

Notes   241

About the Author   243

PREFACE

ONCE A MAN told me that while he can bear to be away from his wife for a couple of days, he can't be without his cellphone for even a moment. His cellphone, it seems, has become dearer than his own family.

What he said reflects our modern predicament: affection between people fades while dependence on external objects grows. In the past, if an ordinary person could lead a carefree life in a comfortable environment, he or she wouldn't have too many other material desires. Today, however, we're bombarded with information, and temptations come at us from all directions. Every single person is so busy both externally and internally, but in the end, do we even know what on earth we were so busy with?

Rather than busying ourselves endlessly with the pursuit of this and that, it makes much better sense to calm ourselves and find true contentment. Now is the time to find the wisdom that brings calmness back to our mind. Fortunately, we need not search further than the Buddha's teachings for this.

Buddhism, though ancient, has never and will never become outdated. It has and will always emanate vigor and wisdom, just like a panacea with time-honored efficacy.

To help more people understand this wisdom, in recent years I've visited over a hundred universities in order to share my thirty years of thoughts and realizations concerning the Buddhadharma. I've offered advice on how to face life's many twists and turns, and in the process have enjoyed numerous heart-to-heart exchanges with students and professors.

Many people have given me positive feedback on my talks and repeatedly asked me to write a book. So, based on some of my lectures and question-and-answer sessions, I've compiled this book for each of you in this busy world. Through this, may you attain the inner peace that Buddhism describes, become less meaninglessly busy, and live with greater calm and self-confidence.

Sodargye

1. MEDITATION AND WEALTH

What hinders us isn't wealth itself but our attachment to it.

SOME OF YOU may think, "Meditation is a Buddhist topic while wealth is secular. In one we are to give up attachment, while in the other we are to forge ahead with determination. How can these two ever become integrated?"

It's actually not so complicated. The management of any business is ultimately the management of the mind. If you can manage your own mind through meditation, you can successfully manage wealth and business with ease.

Everyone longs for success. But what's the criterion for it? True success isn't merely enjoying wealth, status, or fame; instead, it's the ability to rein in your mind and always feel content. This success is relatively easy to achieve through meditation.

What is meditation? Early Buddhist terms for meditation stem from the Sanskrit root *dhyai*, meaning to contemplate or meditate. One definition of meditation given in the Sixth Patriarch's *Platform Sutra* states that meditation involves becoming free from characterization externally and disturbance internally. More simply, it involves keeping your mind calm, away from the disturbances of external objects.

If our minds are constantly disturbed by complex emotions such as restlessness, anxiety, grief, and even excitement rising one after another, it's not difficult to surmise that in all likelihood our actions and decisions will be misguided. In contrast, the choices made with a calm mind are most often wise and well thought out.

Here is a common experience: a person argues fiercely and incoherently with someone, but once they have calmed down after a couple of days, they start to feel regretful and think, "Oh, I was angry when I spoke so irresponsibly the other day. What can I do to fix this situation?" It's much better to avoid regrettable speech and actions in the first place than to try to placate someone afterward. Forming a habit of meditation is the best way to avoid this kind of mistake.

Routinely we wash after getting up in the morning and before going to bed at night. If our bodies need such sanitary care, our minds are certainly no different, so why not give those a cleanup every day too? If we form a habit of meditation, mental trash won't accumulate nor bring too much harm.

In the *Great Treatise on the Perfection of Wisdom* (*Mahaprajna-paramita Shastra*), the Indian Buddhist master Nagarjuna tells us, "Meditation is the pure water that can clean up the dust of desire; meditation is the vajra armor that can protect against the arrows of afflictive emotions."

The *Shurangama Sutra* explains why this is: "When crazy minds come to rest, that rest is enlightenment." Our mind is like the ocean. The moon's reflection doesn't appear when the billows surge, but instead when the ocean is calm. Similarly, when our mind is restless and discursive thoughts rise one after another, wisdom can't appear. It's only when the mind is calmed through meditation that pristine enlightenment can peek through. Basically, when the mind reaches a truly peaceful state, the truth of phenomena can be perceived. If you doubt this, try meditating for a while tonight, and during this process, you might be able to realize something you hadn't noticed before.

Although in the strictest sense, true meditation involves abiding in the nature of Dharma, for ordinary beings and ordinary purposes such as avoiding losing our temper, meditation can also mean constantly keeping a calm mind whether in a vehicle, an office, or at home, or more broadly, whether moving, standing, sitting, or lying down.

Thus, we can delineate two categories of meditation: secular and supramundane meditation.

Secular meditation is the basic form of meditation just described, and it's completely possible to master it as long as we're willing to dedicate ourselves to it. By contrast, supramundane meditation is profound and highly advanced. Great practitioners such as Master Huineng (638–713) from China, Jetsun Milarepa (1040–1123) from Tibet, and Nagarjuna (second century) have reached it. This kind of meditation seems far beyond our ability and its mastery may not be ensured even if we spare no effort on it in this life.

Supramundane meditation results in understanding the truth of all phenomena. There are two approaches to this: the first is to rely on one's own wisdom and instructions from a teacher and go through a long search for the truth, and the second is to rely on meditation to achieve the subtlest state of mind, which lets our pristine wisdom reveal itself. Many Zen masters follow the latter approach. For example, the Sixth Patriarch Huineng was not literate, let alone erudite. Yet through the power of meditation, he attained great enlightenment and unsurpassable wisdom.

If you're interested in meditation, there are some classical sutras on this topic: The *Diamond Sutra* (*Vajracchedika Prajnaparamita Sutra*), *Lotus Sutra* (*Saddharma Pundarika Sutra*), and *Shurangama Sutra*. But reading sutras alone isn't enough. Meditate for a while and look at your mind. If you do this daily, there's a chance that you'll recognize the nature of mind gradually.

Meditation benefits body, mind, and business.

Modern people are saddled with misfortune even though in many places material conditions are excellent. The progress made in just the last few decades is astounding—even my favorite childhood candies are nothing in the eyes of modern children. But sadly people's minds aren't as calm as they were before. Anxiety, restlessness, and depression are pervasive.

Especially in this era of commercialization, everyone is chasing the maximization of wealth. However, impermanence is inevitable in this world; during periods of good fortune, some people make vast amounts of money in a single day, yet if their luck runs out, they can lose everything overnight. How many people can calmly face such ups and downs?

Why are most people so busy these days? For no other reason than to find happiness. Yet while chasing happiness, they too often encounter the opposite: They have too much to do and they face too much stress in their jobs. They actually have countless troubles.

Meditation is the best panacea. It has immense effects on our body and mind. I've seen again and again how people have profoundly changed their minds and health through meditation. Not just me—researchers around the world have discovered the same. For example, in his article "The Effect of Meditation," Professor Shinji Sato at the University of Kyoto in Japan shows that meditation is able to subdue emotions and enhance critical thinking and endurance.

If we can manage to meditate for a couple of minutes to rest our minds after waking up in the morning and before going to bed at night, we'll become increasingly more positive, peaceful, and pleasant, to the extent that even our dreams will be improved. Otherwise, without such practice, we can't experience genuine happiness, no matter how wealthy, powerful, successful, or beautiful we might be.

Meditation benefits us both mentally and physically. Although it can't prevent aging or death, it can give us a stronger constitution. In his "Study of New Medical Meditation," the Japanese doctor Usaburo Hasegawa shows that meditation can help treat twelve different diseases, including high blood pressure, gallstones, tuberculosis, gastroptosis, and insomnia.

Other medical scientists have also concluded that our state of mind can directly affect our physical health. There are many stories like this: checkup reports were mixed up in a medical center and a person who didn't have cancer believed he did and finally became sick due to his negative mental state, whereas a person who did have cancer believed that his cancer was gone and recovered.

Like much of the rest of the world, China today is an aging society, and people pay great attention to how they can enhance the quality of life of the elderly. Many senior citizens have abundant material support but are unhappy because of loneliness. While having a sense of community is very important, if the elderly could dedicate themselves to meditation and keep an eye on their minds, they wouldn't feel so lonely or bored, and their health would improve too.

It has been reported that in the US there are an increasing number of people over the age of sixty have senile dementia. Meditation can also prevent and sometimes even cure this ailment of aging. This is because our brains can be stimulated by meditation, which in turn activates our critical thinking, calms the mind, and strengthens memories. One of my spiritual teachers is over eighty years old this year, but through the power of meditation, his thinking is so sharp and his brain is so clear that he just finished composing a great Buddhist work of three hundred thousand words.

On the Qinghai-Tibet Plateau, you can often see people in their seventies, eighties, and even over one hundred years old, yet they're in great physical condition. Materially speaking, Tibet is far behind China and much of the modern world, but due in part to the people's habits of meditation and mantra chanting, their minds are relatively purer, so many diseases are directly or indirectly prevented, and they have great health and longevity.

After some decades, we'll all be senior citizens. When our time comes, how will we feel? Isn't it better to think about this beforehand? If we get a chance to explore the profound relationship between meditation and the mind and body, we will be tremendously benefited by it.

Through meditation, many have achieved not only the benefits just mentioned, but also success in their businesses and personal endeavors. This is because when the mind is calm, our intuitions become much clearer. Who's able to achieve this state? The answer is anybody, without exception.

A great number of philosophers, writers, and scientists have achieved great things in their fields thanks to what we call meditation. Why? The restless mind understands things at a superficial level. Only when the mind is calm and enters a subtle state similar to meditation can higher levels be reached.

A modern example of someone who has benefited greatly from meditation is Steve Jobs's, the former CEO of Apple. When people talk about Steve Jobs' success, meditation often comes up in the discussion as well. He reportedly meditated every day, which provided him with inspiration and better decision-making strategies. Before making any major decision, he would meditate for a while. We can see the great success he achieved, and I'm sure meditation played a part.

Steve Jobs isn't the only example of a successful businessperson who benefited from meditation. William George, a current Goldman Sachs board member and a former chief executive of the healthcare giant Medtronic, started meditating in 1974. Before deciding on an important investment, he meditates. While traveling by plane, he meditates. Having directly experienced the benefits of meditation, he encouraged his employees to meditate and even turned one of the company's conference rooms into a meditation room.

Many corporations in the US and Europe have their own meditation rooms. They understand that material stimulus alone doesn't lead to strong results. A good business culture, especially one that encourages meditation, can greatly improve workers' enthusiasm and productivity.

Once I was asked by an executive, "Doesn't meditation require solitude? If our corporation initiates it, won't it affect our business?" In fact, meditation doesn't require you to shut down your company and sit all day long. It can be beautifully integrated into life and work and make everything more enjoyable. Unfortunately, many people don't understand this, and everyone suffers as a result.

Does it feel like you're too busy to find happiness?

One of the major problems we face is that we make ourselves so busy that we never get a chance to examine our minds. We never find the time to think about how we're living in this world. We never ask ourselves whether chasing after marriage, career, respect, fame, and personal gain is worth so much effort.

Many people make themselves as busy as ants in order to chase fame and personal benefit. When their desires go unsatisfied, they suffer, but even when they're satisfied, new desires emerge one after another, which again causes more suffering. Through this process, many people become exhausted to the point of collapse.

According to a conservative statistic, in the last twenty years more than 1,200 major entrepreneurs have died by suicide. What was the reason? They had relatively vulnerable minds and didn't understand impermanence or the interdependence of fortune and misfortune.

Fortune and misfortune aren't static. When you're in terrible pain, everything looks hopeless, but after a while, a light at the end of the tunnel may appear. Likewise, when you're extremely successful, even the sunshine seems more brilliant, but this kind of splendor can vanish overnight. As we have seen, when celebrities are at their prime, countless people surround them and serve them, but once they have faded, who bothers to help? This happens in our lives too, so we need to find some sort of inner strength.

If we value meditation, it's extremely helpful for strengthening our minds. I knew an old practitioner who had been imprisoned for twenty-one years during the Cultural Revolution. He said it was a wonderful opportunity for practice. During that time, nobody bothered him, so he could meditate freely, his mind was cheerful, and he was able to face adversity calmly. However, after he was released, people showed him tremendous respect and made offerings to him. After meeting with so many people and dealing with so many trivial matters, his spiritual state wasn't as great as before. The point is that it's worth contemplating what's truly valuable in our lives.

Money is both viper and gold.

Almost everyone would agree that having money is a good thing. But while money has its positive side, it also has its flip side.

For instance, many families who don't have much money get along wonderfully, but once they get rich, their relationships can deteriorate and various conflicts emerge one after another. Indeed, sometimes money brings more problems than we can imagine.

There's a Buddhist sutra about the trouble with money: One day when going out to beg for food, the Buddha and his attendant Ananda saw a piece of gold on the roadside. The Buddha said, "Viper." Ananda took a look and also said, "Viper." Then they left.

Out of curiosity, a nearby peasant who overheard them went over to take a look and found that their viper was actually gold. Elated, he exclaimed, "How stupid you monks are! If you don't take it, I'll take it!" He excitedly picked it up and went home.

From then on, this peasant never went to work in the fields, instead amusing himself with friends day after day. But after a short while, he was involved in a lawsuit and sent to prison because of this piece of gold. Then he understood: gold is a viper.

Money is complicated. When we have it, we must have the correct perception of it. Only then can we properly manage it.

Over 2,500 years ago, the Buddha explained how to manage wealth in great detail. In the *Sigalovada Sutta*, the Buddha advised that we take 50 percent of our income to reinvest in business, use 25 percent for living expenses, and reserve 25 percent for contingencies.

It's sad that many people don't understand this. They invest hotheadedly without a reasonable plan, they're blindly optimistic about every opportunity without considering the risk, and they end up bankrupt. Even more unfortunate are the people who act as if they were great gamblers. With little initial capital, they impulsively invest with substantive loans, lose everything without the ability to repay, and end up taking their own lives.

Wisdom is needed to manage wealth. Always expect the best, but plan for the worst. Ask this question about all endeavors: What if I fail?

Seventy percent of your income will be spent by others.

Even if we're astute in business, wise in managing our wealth, and accumulate a sufficient means for living, it's important to remember that it doesn't belong just to us.

A Buddhist sutra says that wealth is shared by five owners: the king and ministers can take it by law, robbers can take it by breaking the law, nonfilial offspring can squander it through negligence, others can share it, and natural disasters can take it away. Furthermore, after we die, we can't be sure where the money we have accumulated through so much effort will go.

The other day, I read a thought-provoking post online. It said that 70 percent of the functions on a smartphone are useless. In a luxurious mansion, 70 percent of the space is vacant. In a closet full of beautiful clothes, 70 percent are rarely if ever worn. Whatever amount of money we might earn in this life, 70 percent of it will be spent by others.

Therefore, having exerted ourselves and exhausted ourselves for our entire life, what we can enjoy for ourselves is a mere 30 percent. Understanding this, we should spend our money on meaningful things while we still have the chance.

What are these meaningful things?

Acts that help others.

Certainly, most people can't follow the examples of Bill Gates and Sir Li Ka-shing, who have spent half of their assets on charity. However, if you make a comfortable living, wouldn't it be okay to take fifty or a hundred dollars to help others?

If you don't trust charitable organizations, you can skip them and just do it by yourself. Never give up your loving heart because of a lack of trust.

In the places where we usually pay no attention, there are so many poor people. An amount of money that means nothing to you could actually change the lives of some of these individuals. With your support, a needy child could have a chance to be educated and lead a completely different life, or a patient who's fighting to survive but can't afford the medical bills might have his or her life extended. There are so many beings in need. We can certainly find somebody to help. Happiness is built on altruism, so aspire to benefit sentient beings with real action.

To conclude, my advice to each of you is to meditate and be generous with your wealth. The value of meditating or hoarding wealth only for your own benefit is very small. We don't seek buddhahood for our own happiness alone. By meditating I hope you can calm your surging thoughts and desires and perhaps even realize the nature of all phenomena. Then you'll be able to truly benefit all sentient beings.

Q&A

How do I meditate?
One Buddhist saying goes: "Reciting the names of buddhas does not rely on the lips; meditating does not depend on the legs." Form isn't important—mind is the key. Nonetheless, appropriate posture can improve the effect of meditation. When meditating, you can follow the seven-point posture of Vairochana: cross the legs so that the backs of the feet rest on the thigh of the opposite leg, place the hands in the lap, palms up, with the right hand on top of the left, straighten the body, relax the shoulders (keeping them outward, not inward), slightly tilt the head downward, keep the eyes slightly open, and touch the tongue to the roof of the mouth.

This posture helps to subdue the mind.

If we can meditate every day for five to ten minutes after waking up and for five to ten minutes before going to bed, our restless minds will gradually become calmer.

In monasteries, I often see the words "Nondual Dharma Gate." Would you please explain the meaning of "Nondual"?

"Nondual" means having transcended the paradoxes of dualism, such as existence and nonexistence, right and wrong. This is the state of enlightenment, which is inconceivable; it's neither "existence" nor "nonexistence," and it's beyond thoughts and words.

How can we embody the statement, "Reciting the names of buddhas does not rely on the lips; meditating does not depend on the legs"?

This statement is given in an ultimate sense. For beginners, it's better to sit cross-legged for meditation and recite the names of buddhas clearly, one by one. However, at the most advanced level, formality isn't necessary. As long as you don't forget to watch your mind at all times, then walking, standing, sitting, and lying down are all forms of meditation.

My understanding is that meditative concentration is a state of realization and meditation is the process that brings you there. Is this correct?

Yes, meditative concentration is indeed a state of realization. It can be basic or advanced. There are four kinds of meditation and eight categories of concentration in a secular sense, as well as the supramundane concentration of abiding in the nature of emptiness. The aim of meditation is to reach these states.

Nowadays there are many descriptions of meditation. It has even been applied to tea and the stock market. Buddhism has the potential to be integrated into every aspect of our life, but you have to savor the real taste of meditation for yourself.

I want to improve my language skills. How can we speak confidently and frankly with our mind and brain working in harmony? Which one do you rely on when you speak?
Without using the brain, we don't know what to say; without using the heart, our words won't resonate with others.

Scholars speak with their brain while practitioners speak with their minds. How do these differ? When speaking with the brain, we don't speak from our own experience but instead repeat things we've already heard; when speaking with our mind, we may not use a lot of examples but instead express our understanding through our own realizations and observations.

I'm trying to follow the latter. In fact, I use both when I talk, but mainly my mind.

What I've said today comes from the depths of my heart. I really hope that through meditation your exhausted minds can find comfort and ease and that you can avoid being so busy. Only when your mind is peaceful can you be genuinely happy.

Lecture at Peking University
July 14, 2012

2. WHAT IS LOVE?

If the Buddha were asked how to deal with romantic love, he wouldn't encourage everybody to renounce the householder's life nor would he ask everyone to follow Buddhism. He would say: "Don't become too obsessed with it. Otherwise you'll suffer in a cocoon spun by yourself rather than by someone else."

As a MONK, it may seem like I'm making a fool of myself by talking about love and affection to "experts" like all of you. However, I've been to many universities and witnessed with great sadness young people living and dying for love and making romantic love their first priority. So many university students aren't at all sober when it comes to romantic love. Some may obtain the highest degrees possible but have no sense of the keys to a good relationship, and some even rashly give up their lives when facing small relationship issues. How can they make their years of academic study meaningful? Clearly they haven't recognized the true face of love. In fact, helping young people obtain a more authentic understanding of life and what "love" is in particular has driven me to speak at universities like this one.

When I was young, I also had desire and attachment. Now, I can't say that I have any realization, but through contemplating real stories that have happened in the past and through examining the mind with Buddhadharma, I've gained an authentic understanding of the essence of affection and have gradually freed myself from its confusion.

Some people may think, "How can Buddhist monks understand love? You guys are so cold-hearted that you forsake your loved ones in order to lead a monastic life!" In fact, the Buddhist attitude toward love isn't heartless or cold, but instead warns people about the dangers of romantic love and the dreariness of attachment. If love were perfect in every way, it would only bring happiness and would obviously be worth praising. Unfortunately, the fact is that so many hidden causes of suffering are behind and within it. This is expounded both in traditional culture and Buddhist scriptures.

Young people really need a correct understanding of this. If you can come to understand it better, then even if you may have desire, it will not bring you agony or make you want to die.

There is misery in love.

Love isn't as beautiful as you think. It's not as magnificent as all the fictitious romantic wrappers make it seem. Even so, many people become enthralled and even go insane until one day, when the wrapper is torn off, they painfully discover what love really is. Romantic love is just like a bubble that can't withstand a gentle touch, let alone a windstorm. Without recognizing this, people become upset, desperate, and even commit suicide.

Take this story, for example: In the Southern dynasty, Liu Zhen's[1] younger sister was married to Emperor Po Yang[2] and they had a perfect married life. However, for unclear reasons, Emperor Po Yang was eventually put to death. His wife was desperately heartbroken, bedridden, and almost died. Upon hearing about his sister's dire situation, Liu Zhen asked a painter to draw a picture of Emperor Po Yang intimately holding a beautiful woman in his arms while looking at himself in a mirror. Once the painting was shown to her, Liu Zhen's sister flew into a rage and felt that he was unworthy of her grief and quickly recovered. If just a fabricated picture can turn a fervent love into anger, what does this say about love?

Love is fragile and impermanent. The Buddhist text *Four Hundred Stanzas on the Middle Way* states that impermanent objects are subject to change, and changing objects keep people from peace and happiness; therefore, the nature of any impermanent object is suffering.

We all know this. We know that romantic love has a shelf life, which is often very short. I've read some statistics that suggest that romantic attraction lasts from three months up to three years. Once the expiration date is reached, the couple feels less attracted to each other, and as time goes by, they often find more problems and shortcomings in their partner. This is why the Buddha repeatedly told us: love seems extremely intriguing, but what's concealed within it is impermanence and misery.

Some of you may not agree with me. However, if you have never experienced the ups and downs of romantic love, it's normal to have doubts. But for those of you who have gone through this once, twice, or many times, you must have a very good sense of it, and I'm sure you understand exactly what I'm saying.

Romantic love is a form of strong attachment, so it's bound to cause suffering. When you fall in love with someone, you feel romantic and content at first. But as time goes on, since it's an impermanent phenomenon, this sentiment changes and you find suffering overtaking happiness. Even if you spend a lifetime enraptured with each other, you can't accompany each other beyond this lifetime, so the separation will certainly bring suffering.

The *Amitayus Sutra* says, "In this world of love and lust, people are born alone and die alone, come alone and leave alone." We were born by ourselves and will die without companions. Nobody will accompany us forever; thus, never hold the view that "without him or her, I couldn't survive." Some people understand this, but they're unwilling to accept it. Ironically, the more you fear losing what you hold on to, the more likely it is to happen.

At the ultimate level of emptiness, there's no phenomenon that inherently exists, and love is no exception. Since love doesn't inherently exist, if we take it as a permanent refuge or the key to lasting happiness, we will just fall further into delusion and misery. This is all but guaranteed when love doesn't live up to our expectations, or when we're separated from the objects of our affection.

It's actually the love of "I."

When in love, people like to make oaths of eternal devotion. But however pleasant these might sound, the person making the oath always loves him or herself most. When their partner makes them happy, they want to be together from dawn to dusk. Once they're betrayed, however, their love turns to animosity.

In Hong Kong there was a girl who told her boyfriend that she wanted to end their relationship. But the boy wasn't ready. When the girl insisted, the boy killed her. With a sharp knife, he stabbed her heart over ten times and then decapitated her. Afterward, a news reporter asked him, "She was already dead. Why did you cut off her head?" Coldly, he replied, "I wanted to make sure she was really dead."

It's said that romantic love is the ultimate state of human selfishness. In any romantic relationship, people say "I" love you, but it's actually due to grasping at an "I" that love comes to be. Every effort is for "I," not for love.

We're only flesh and bones.

The Buddha told his disciples to stop depending on their deluded thoughts because they're unreliable. He also told them to give up craving for women, or else there will be endless misfortune. As one sutra says, "Be cautious about believing in your own thoughts, because they are always unreliable; be cautious about meeting with women, because they will bring disaster." Here we can understand "women" to mean a person to whom we feel great attraction.

When people think that someone is beautiful and attractive, it's actually just a delusion. If you analyze this attraction with wisdom, you'll easily find that what you're so fond of is in reality a pile of bones and flesh. The next time you feel attracted to someone, consider the things that make up that person's physical form. You'll come to your senses and realize, "What I'm loving and longing for is just blood, bones, and flesh."

There's a great master in Thailand called Ajahn Chah. Once, when sitting in a car with two monks from the West, he suddenly turned back to the American monk and said, "You are thinking of your girl-friend in Los Angeles."

That monk was rather embarrassed.

Ajahn Chah continued, "You write to her and ask her to send you a very personal item, so you can take a look at it when you miss her."

The American monk curiously asked, "Am I allowed to do this as a monk?"

Ajahn Chah said, "Of course! Ask her to send you a bottle of her feces; every time you miss her, take it out and smell it."

It sounds like a joke, but Ajahn Chah was telling him the universal truth of the impurity of human bodies, not only the bodies of women but also men's bodies.

Long ago when Matangi's daughter fell in love with Ananda, a cousin of the Buddha, she went to see the Buddha and requested that he tell Ananda to give up his monastic precepts and marry her. The Buddha asked, "What makes you love him?"

Obsessed, she said, "I love his bright eyes, handsome nose, charming ears, sweet voice, and elegance. I just love everything about him."

The Buddha told her, "In Ananda's eyes, there is mucus; in his nose, there is snot; in his mouth, there is saliva; in his ears, there is wax; in his body, there are feces and urine. Which one do you love?" The Buddha then asked an attendant to bring a pot of dirty water from Ananda's bath and said to her, "Since you deeply love Ananda, how about you drink it?"

Overwhelmed and having carefully examined the Buddha's words, Matangi's daughter found they really made sense to her, and her strong craving suddenly was quenched.

What makes you love?

Why do so many people make romantic love the focus of their lives?

Romantic relationships are fairly subtle. If we only look at this life without thinking of past lives, many phenomena are difficult to explain. Scientists such as the biological anthropologist Helen Fisher have spent decades asking questions like these: Why do we fall in love with someone at first sight? Why are we attracted to one person and not another? She found that three basic drives—lust, attraction, and attachment—are related to reproduction. Each is associated with different chemicals in the brain and each interacts with the others.

From the Buddhist point of view, relationships aren't an accident. They're due to previous unfinished connections. So, your partner comes to you either to return your kindness or to demand satisfaction. If you deny this law of karmic cause and effect, there will be confusion when facing relationship issues.

In Tibet, people recognize the law of karmic cause and effect and so they seek romantic love, but they don't excessively praise it or take it to be everything in life. Previously, there were no equivalent terms for words like "lovelorn" or phrases like "to die for love" in Tibetan languages, but as foreign movies and television shows become increasingly popular in Tibet, the younger generations have started to become confused by love.

In other parts of the world, few people give any thought to previous lives or the law of karmic cause and effect, and romantic love is embellished to the ultimate extent. Just think about the poems, novels, works of art, music, movies, and television shows of the past and today, many of which involve romantic love and affection. We're told that romantic love is the greatest kind of magic. Consider, for example, how many versions there are of this story alone: In ancient Greece, the sculptor Pygmalion fell in love with a stone sculpture of a girl that he had sculpted. He was so obsessed that he couldn't help watching and taking care of her day and night, and finally proposed to her. Having been deeply moved, the sculpture gained life, and without hesitation, ran into his arms. Stories like this influence people to think that romantic love is something miraculous that can make their lives perfect.

Finding the love of the Buddha.

If the Buddha were asked how to deal with romantic love, he wouldn't encourage everybody to renounce the householder's life nor would he ask everyone to follow Buddhism. He would say: "Don't become too obsessed with it. Otherwise you'll suffer in a cocoon spun by yourself rather than by someone else."

At the conventional level, the Buddha didn't oppose a normal life that includes a romantic relationship. He didn't blindly reject romantic love. In the *Samyuktagama*, the *Ekottaragama Sutra*, and the *Sigalovada Sutta*, the Buddha gave detailed discourses on the ethical courtesies for husbands and wives so that they can get along well with each other. He didn't encourage everybody to give up love and renounce a householder's life.

Of course, he himself did leave the palace, his wife, and son. He renounced the householder's life. This sacrifice of love and affection wasn't irresponsible, nor was it for his individual liberation. Instead, it was to find a way to free sentient beings from suffering. This is the true meaning of love. The Buddha demonstrated true love by giving up everything he knew and cared about in order to bring lasting happiness to all beings.

Compared with selfish love, the love of the Buddha is unconditional, and the object of his love is all sentient beings. Some people may think this is impossible, but this is indeed the love advocated in Buddhist traditions. Not only does the Buddha have it, but every individual is able to develop it. Over two thousand years ago, the Buddha realized and articulated his path of love and compassion, which brings all beings out of suffering. By contrast, scientific innovations can enhance the material world, but they can't necessarily make everyone happier.

To conclude, if everyone understood Buddhist secrets for taming the mind, they would very likely reach happiness and freedom. Setting aside the exalted goal of reaching Buddhahood or freeing sentient beings, we should understand some basic Buddhadharma even just to lead a better life with a more sensible attitude. We should always think about basic Buddhist teachings like "everything is impermanent." I hope you can spend some of your spare time contemplating the significance of this.

Many young people bustle about, feverishly pursuing love, fame, and personal gain, and never pause to think about life's end. Only when the last moment arrives do they start to worry, "Will my life continue after I die? What will I become in my next life?" However, at that point, it's too late to ponder over this.

Today, I only want to remind you that while you're chasing romantic love, be prepared for impermanence. There are many wise instructions on this topic in Buddhism. The *Guide to the Bodhisattva's Way of Life* is an exceptionally fine guide. It teaches us how to give up our self-centered ideas, and how to untie our various attachments. If you get the chance to study it, you'll find proper direction for your life. Remember that if your mind is full of selfishness and attachment, happiness will always be out of reach.

Q&A

Say there are two young people who fall in love with each other, but their families don't want them to be together. They want to consider their family, but they also don't want to give up their love. What should they do?

When family and romantic love conflict, I suppose the best way is to make every effort to talk with your families and avoid upsetting them. But protect your love as well. This kind of conflict can't be resolved in a short time. Nevertheless, you shouldn't be impulsive. As long as you make an effort, there will be a better result.

In reality, many parents aren't happy about their children's choices in the beginning. But through mediation, they begin to accept things gradually. This happens often.

You mentioned that romantic love brings suffering only because of attachment, and if we give up attachment, there won't be any more suffering. How about attachment to chasing virtue? Will it cause suffering too? Should we give it up?

There are two kinds of attachment. One causes suffering, such as attachment to romantic love and wealth. These things aren't as worthwhile as we think. When we become attached in these ways, suffering follows.

The other type of attachment doesn't cause suffering. This includes seeking virtuous practice and benefiting others. Such things are indeed forms of attachment and need to be given up when we reach the highest levels of realization, but we do need them temporarily.

These are comparable to two kinds of boats. One is safe and can ferry you across a river. When you reach the other shore, you can abandon it. But when you're still on the river, the boat is indispensable. The other type is unsafe. It can't ferry you across the river, and in fact it puts you in danger, so you need to keep away from it.

Similarly, our attachments can be positive or negative. We can make use of positive attachments temporarily and give them up in the end. But in the case of negative attachments, we have to give them up right away.

The Buddha said that all phenomena are empty, but a Mahayana Buddhist teacher has the bodhichitta required to benefit all sentient beings. Does this mean that "affection" still exists in their heart?

Once a Mahayana practitioner realizes that everything is empty, he or she will naturally give up all attachments. But before then, generating bodhichitta and benefiting sentient beings is indispensable for the process. Such "affection" doesn't hinder spiritual growth.

Is realizing the nature of emptiness for benefiting sentient beings or oneself? The wise will definitely choose the former. In fact, only when you eliminate self-attachment can the luminous nature of mind be successfully recognized.

On the path to enlightenment, we must clearly understand the relationship between the emptiness of all phenomena and the work of benefiting all sentient beings. We should know that at the ultimate level, everything is unfindable, while at the phenomenal level, everything appears in front of us.

Ultimately, everything is unreal, just like in a dream. But before we wake up, we still try to eliminate suffering and chase happiness. In the same way, from the standpoint of emptiness, benefiting sentient beings is also a dream, but before enlightenment is reached, don't give it up!

Lecture at Xiamen University
February 23, 2012

3. Science and the Path to Happiness

Some people believe that religion contradicts science. As a scientific researcher, I recognize that science can prove the existence of something but not its nonexistence.

What is science?

FIRST, LET'S DEFINE science. There are various definitions and descriptions of it, but most basically, science should objectively reflect the truth of all phenomena. Science falls into two categories: natural science and social science. Recently cognitive science has also flourished, which focuses on exploring the profound mysteries of the mind.

Researchers have made great progress in the first two categories. To some extent, they have discovered the ways in which many aspects of this world operate, such as the law of gravity, the theory of relativity, and quantum mechanics. The field of mind science, however, only began at the end of the last century, and it hasn't yet drawn as much public attention.

Recently more and more people in the West have become interested in cognitive science. Some scholars have found that certain things the Buddha describes in the canonical literature match current scientific findings and that the Buddhist teachings correspond to scientific discoveries about the nature of our cognitive life.

What has science brought to human beings?

Materially, science has offered us tremendous conveniences. In ancient times, and even only a few decades ago, we had no internet, cellphones, or computers. But now these technologies are changing our lives at a remarkable pace. In certain ways, science and technology have benefited mankind tremendously.

Yet technology is a double-edged sword. Without control, it can lead to unimaginable disasters. The two world wars in the last century clearly prove this. Although catastrophes on such a large scale haven't occurred more recently, the insecurity caused by the drawbacks of science and technology is pervasive.

Ancient people were aware of this, and some even opposed the development of science and technology. In ancient China there existed very advanced technology. For instance, some sources claim that toward the end of the Period of Spring and Autumn, Lu Ban built prototypes of an automobile and an airplane.[3] Duan Chengshi's *Miscellaneous Morsels from Youyang* records that Lu Ban made a wooden glider that flew for three days before descending. Once his father snuck into it and after a single flight found himself at Su Zhou, a city quite far away. As stated in Wang Cong's *Discourses Weighed in the Balance*, his mother also once got onto a wooden horse that he had made, and "it drove her away without return. His mother was lost."

Why haven't these technologies been passed down to later generations?

Some argue that people in ancient China believed that excess attention to trivial things saps the will. Especially in Confucianism, the "path" is the key; only the inferior are infatuated with "instruments." It's said that "metaphysics is the path, while physics is the instrument." However, modern people have lost sight of this, focusing only on science and technology. Thanks to technological advancements, they seem to live very comfortably, but only they themselves know their inner confusion.

Influenced by modernity, some Tibetan nomads long for the lifestyle of those in the Chinese areas. They spend all their savings on a down payment for an apartment in the city and view it as the greatest glory of their life. By contrast, many people in the Chinese areas are tired of a life of luxury and dissipation—not to mention heavy traffic—so they wish to get away from the hustle and bustle and long for the lifestyle of those living in the Tibetan areas. This interesting phenomenon reflects what the twentieth-century Chinese author Qian Zhongshu describes in Fortress Besieged: "People outside desperately push into the city; people inside the city desperately run out."

In fact, whether people are inside or outside of the city, whatever they do is only for happiness. Unfortunately, nowadays, the causes of unhappiness have increasingly multiplied in daily life.

A recent report stated that the world's population reached a new high of seven billion on October 31, 2011. It took one hundred years for the population to increase from one billion to two billion, thirty years for it to rise from two billion to three billion, and as little as twenty years to rise from five billion to seven billion. The earth's capacity is limited, and as the population continuously expands, crises over natural resources, ecology, and environmental pollution have become more and more severe. The earth has become overloaded.

Some nations have taken the measure of state-dictated "birth control" in an attempt to mitigate the problem. However, such circumstances cause young people to be burdened with more pressure to give up hopes of a family life and instead focus only on making money. I've been to many universities and found that a great number of students were pondering how to make money instead of focusing on their studies. If this is the case for the younger generation, what will our future society become?

Of course, sometimes, the mentality of students is also influenced by their teacher. A professor from Peking Normal University told his graduate students, "If you can't make forty million yuan before you reach forty years old, don't come to see me." This story caused a stir after it was reported. Someone commented that since his students were in real estate, in order to make forty million yuan, they would have to do the following four things: ensure sudden, huge profits; be merciless in their dealings; bribe people; and aggressively pull down existing buildings. Only by doing these four things could someone make forty million yuan before reaching the age of forty. What's the driving idea behind these four behaviors? Profit above all else.

Many people will stop at nothing to make money. Take gutter oil[+] for example. This has become a quick way to make a fortune. According to some data, around three million tons of gutter oil has been sent to dinner tables each year in China. The annual profit of the gutter oil business is close to two billion yuan. The toxicity of such low-quality oil is one hundred times that of white arsenic; it's extremely harmful to human health.

The Buddha said that if one commits negative karma joyfully, the result will ultimately be experienced mournfully. As it's said in the *Sutra of the Sublime Dharma of Clear Recollection*, "When such misdeeds were committed, one was joyfully laughing, but when the misfortunes ripen, one wails while experiencing it."

What is happiness?

Some people may ask, "If money can't bring happiness, then what's happiness exactly?"

From the Buddhist point of view, with inner contentment, one feels happy even when penniless. Yet if their desires are insatiable, even extremely wealthy people will have no chance of feeling happy.

The *Sutra on the Buddha's Bequeathed Teaching* said, "People with contentment feel happy even when they have to sleep on the floor; people without contentment feel unhappy even when they are in heaven." Happiness, then, is a sense of inner contentment, and has very little to do with external circumstances.

Einstein once said, "Human knowledge and skills alone cannot lead humanity to a happy and dignified life." Socrates also argued that virtue is knowledge. In order to attain happiness, we should first pursue knowledge and then practice virtue and accumulate merit.

When pursuing knowledge, we should pursue the knowledge associated with spiritual wisdom. Only this knowledge can bring us lasting happiness. If you understand Buddhism's profound meaning, you're benefited in this present life and in future lives.

Nowadays, many people are interested in Buddhism, which is very good because if you expect to gain happiness from wealth, you'll only become increasingly miserable. Why? Desire is infinite. Even if you possess the wealth of the entire world, it won't necessarily satisfy you. A Buddhist sutra states, "Worldly people are insatiable; even when you gain everything that you desire, you are still unsatisfied."

No matter how much you own, what you can enjoy is very limited. An old saying goes, "Even if you possess thousands of mansions, you need at most seven feet for sleeping at night; even if you own thousands of acres of fertile land, what you can consume each day is at most three liters." Thus, we should abandon our ambitions for grand living and give up pursuing unneeded things.

Life is precious; why not use it to pursue wisdom and moral conduct? Without these two, even if we possess power, fame, wealth, and talent, we'll still be unhappy. The novelist and essayist Jin Yong described such people as, at best, "carefree paupers."

How do we attain happiness?

Buddhism offers various approaches to attain genuine happiness:

1. *Understand that everything follows the law of karmic cause and effect*
From the Buddhist point of view, a carefree life results from the merit you have accumulated in previous lives. If you performed virtuous deeds in your previous lives, then even without much effort in this present life, fame and personal gain will come to you. But without accumulating positive karma, then no matter how hard you work, you'll still find it hard to fulfill your wishes, just as you can't get oil by squeezing sand. Whether you believe this or not, it's the truth.

Our conduct in previous lives directly affects our present life. Similarly, what we'll experience in the next life is determined by our current and past actions. Therefore, our fate isn't governed by others; everything is up to us. We're our own gurus.

Even though few people these days believe in "one good turn deserves another," it's still very true. To judge the veracity of an assumption based on the number of its supporters is at best erroneous—just as the number of people who can't understand advanced scientific theories isn't small, but their ignorance and disagreement can't refute the rationality of science. Previously, most of the Western world believed that the earth was flat, but this belief didn't make it so. Meanwhile, many people may embrace the law of karmic cause and effect, but if they find it inconvenient to follow, they simply won't follow it. Even though most people drive faster than highway speed limits, this doesn't negate the reality that accidents are more common and more often fatal at higher speeds.

2. Adjust your mind and body with meditation

Many research institutes around the world have discovered that when we apply meditation in our daily life, we feel happier.

As early as 1967, Dr. Herbert Benson, from Harvard University, conducted an experiment about meditation. The results suggested that meditation can alleviate stress in the human body.

There was another experiment carried out in a clinical center in America. A group of people were asked to meditate twenty-seven minutes every day for one week, and they were examined using certain instruments before and after. The results showed that their happiness index increased dramatically.

Another research institute examined experienced Tibetan Buddhist meditators with sophisticated instruments. The results showed that after meditation, those meditators' sense of happiness increased by 700 percent, which caused the researchers to question the accuracy of their instruments. They then conducted the same experiment with two groups of university students who had no idea about meditation. One group practiced meditation for a period of time while the other group didn't. The results showed distinctive differences between the two groups.

Nowadays meditation has become popular in mainstream American culture. Over ten million American adults meditate regularly. They may start because it seems cool to meditate, but they'll continue because they see the benefits of it.

Such meditation-based therapy has also drawn widespread attention in regions like Western Europe and Singapore. Today, more and more people have realized that money can't buy inner comfort and ease. Instead they meditate for five minutes or more every day to find inner peace and happiness.

3. Reflect on the meaning of Buddhist theories

If our Dharma study and meditation are only superficial, and we don't alter our thinking patterns, then this is far from enough. This isn't to say that form isn't important. Some people like to take things to the extreme and believe that it's unnecessary to chant prayers, meditate, or take refuge or ordination because these are all formalities. This is mistaken. Under certain circumstances, some formal practice is required. If all such practices were unnecessary, then when people fall in love, why would they take great pains to get marriage certificates and hold wedding ceremonies?

But it isn't enough to focus only on the form of our practice. As Buddhists, we must aim to achieve some degree of inner realization. But even if we can't get to this point, at least we can cultivate a good understanding of Buddhist theories. In this way, over time, afflictive emotions and suffering will decrease.

Zen Master Wumen said, "There are diverse flowers in spring, a beautiful moon in autumn, cool wind in summer, and white snow in winter. When no worry dwells in the mind, it is the good season in the human world." Such happiness is genuine and can't be substituted with driving a luxurious car or wearing name-brand clothes. How is it that so many practitioners living in deserted mountains can greatly enjoy themselves? This is because through long-term meditation, they have attained inner comfort and ease and perceive everything as a dream, unlike worldly people who mistake everything for being intrinsically existent.

When we read the daily news, it's very easy for us to understand the extremely miserable lives of worldly people. What leads to their suffering? Attachment. If we understand that everything is impermanent and empty, then no matter who we are, whether rich or poor, we will experience comfort and ease. Then we can be like the philanthropist Sir Li Ka-shing, who has vast wealth but isn't fettered by it. His life is plain, and he isn't fastidious about his clothing or shoes. It's very common for him to wear the same business suit for eight to ten years. His mother was a Buddhist who taught him the law of karmic cause and effect and encouraged him to do virtuous deeds when he was little. When Sir Li Ka-shing taught his own children, he also used Buddhist theories to inspire them to understand how to be wise. Some say that two-thirds of his words were about how to be good people and one-third was about how to do business. Once, he said, "If the money is mine, I'll bend down to pick it up even if it's just one yuan. However, if it's not mine, even if ten million yuan were sent to my door, I wouldn't take it. Every ten cents I've made can be put on the table."

By contrast, some people make money unscrupulously. The more money they make, the less happy they feel. Whether our life is short or long, when we look back on our lives on our deathbeds, it's best not to have too many sharp pangs of guilt for conscienceless misdeeds.

How extremely beneficial it would be if all we had to do to find the truth of life was live a couple of decades.

Here in Xi'an, the Terracotta Army is world famous and has been called "the Eighth Wonder of the World." Personally, I don't think it's very wonderous. What's the most wonderous thing? The wisdom that the Buddha shared over 2,500 years ago. It reveals the mystery of the universe, the origin of mankind, and the world of the mind, and has been preserved in the Buddhist canonical literature. It's a pity that a historic site like the Terracotta Army is visited by a continuous flow of people every day, while the wisdom that can genuinely benefit all beings is often neglected and has only interested a few people enough to really study it.

These days we keep heading forward in the direction of material progress, but spiritually, we would be better off returning to ancient wisdom. Arnold J. Toynbee said, "Now who are the individuals who are the greatest benefactors of the living generation of mankind? I should say: Confucius and Lao-Tse; the Buddha; the Prophets of Israel and Judah; Zoroaster, Jesus, Muhammad; and Socrates." I particularly hope that in the future, more people will stop confining their studies to natural science and social science, because it's more important for us to find happiness using the science of the mind.

Q&A

On a philosophy exam, there was a question: please refute that you're not in a dream right now. We couldn't find a solution even after a long discussion. Would you please give us a hint?
You're right that you can't find a solution. We're indeed in a dream, just as it's said in the *Diamond Sutra*: "All compounded phenomena are like dreams, illusions, water bubbles, and reflections."

A great Tibetan master Mipham Rinpoché composed a *Debate between Dreaming and Waking*, in which Dreaming and Waking are personified as two characters. They debate who's fake and who's authentic. Most ordinary people would think that Waking should win, but the result isn't that simple.

When I first arrived at our Buddhist institute, our guru, who was like a wish-fulfilling jewel, was teaching on this text. At that time, I had the sense that waking life isn't really different from a dream because I couldn't find a reason to rebuke this view. We may think that what we experience while awake isn't a dream because we can see things and touch them. However, in a dream, we can touch things and feel them exactly as we do while awake. We may think that our waking hours are long and our dreams are short, and thus our dreams are unreal. However, some dreams give us a feeling of passing over an extremely long period of time. We see this with the *Dream of Nanke, A Golden Millet Dream,* and the episode "The Inner Light" in *Star Trek: The Next Generation.*⁵ Regardless of how we look at it, we'll still find that everything we experience while awake is ultimately unreal.

Of course, if you would like to prove this view further, you would have to dive into the Buddhist sutras, especially the *Avatamsaka Sutra* and the *King of Samadhi Sutra.*

I've believed from childhood that Buddhadharma can greatly benefit human beings, and I hope to help people around me with my limited abilities. How should I fulfill this?
First, don't deliberately harm any sentient being, even if it's as small as an ant. Then, on top of that, try to help the people around you and benefit society as much as you can. Of course, we all have different causes and conditions and abilities to benefit others. As long as you have an altruistic heart, it will shine forth.

I don't know much about Buddhism, but I do believe in some basic Buddhist concepts, such as "one good turn deserves another." I would love to live a simple life, but in this city, there are so many negative things, such as gutter oil, toxic baby formula, and jerry-built building projects. Do I have to escape the city?
What you have said is true. Buddhists and intellectuals should exchange ideas. I know some intellectuals hold the karmic principle of "one good turn deserves another" to be true, but their belief in it is confined to the present life, and thus many people expect good results to ripen soon after they have done some virtuous deeds. Concepts like future lives have never occurred to some people.

If we understand that cyclic existence is a very lengthy process, then we'll see that some of the virtuous deeds done in this life may bear results in this lifetime, but the majority may have to wait till many lives later. However, the law of karmic cause and effect never fails, so we must abandon nonvirtue and adopt virtue.

In the present context, there are plenty of occasions for committing misdeeds, but the answer isn't to blindly escape. Instead, we should assume the responsibility of improving circumstances by starting with ourselves.

Of course, you may make some mistakes unconsciously because it's not always easy to be aware of the dark side of our circumstances. Still, if you don't have the intention to do wrong, it's said in Buddhist sutras that the fault isn't too grave, just like killing an insect by accidentally stepping on it.

Buddhadharma is excellent, but the canons of Tibetan Buddhism, Theravada Buddhism, and Chinese Buddhism are voluminous. As ordinary people, how should we study to make Buddhadharma part of our being?
Buddhist sutras are indeed vast. It's impossible to study all of them in such a short life. Fortunately, many great masters of the past have summarized the canonical literature into concise pith instructions in the form of commentaries. If you study them, it's very easy to master the essence of Buddhadharma.

What commentaries are most suitable for us to start with? From my own experience, it's better to study the *Guide to the Bodhisattva's Way of Life* and the *Words of My Perfect Teacher* first.

In the *Words of My Perfect Teacher*, there are thorough explanations of all the stages of practice, from the reflection on the rarity of human existence at the beginning up to the practice that one should perform to be born in the Pure Land of Great Bliss at the end. It's just one book, yet it encompasses all the essential instructions in all the scriptures of Sutrayana and Tantrayana. I've taught on this book in the past couple of years, and what I've said has been transcribed into eight volumes. If you get a chance to study it, you'll clearly comprehend the basic framework of Buddhadharma: How do I take refuge? How do I generate bodhichitta? How do I practice the ten virtuous deeds? How do I decide what to adopt and what to abandon? You'll completely understand all the vital points like these.

It's crucial to systematically study some Buddhist scriptures. Otherwise, your practice will be superficial at best. Without understanding the theories behind it, the foundation of Buddhism is lost.

Our society is experiencing moral degeneration. As a staff member of the Shanxi Moral and Cultural Research Society, I really wish to cultivate myself morally and help society in the same way. What do you think is the best approach?

I'm not sure about the aim and activities of your organization, so my suggestions can't be specific. Generally speaking, though, it's not easy to see immediate effects from any great undertaking of this kind. As long as you persevere and apply modern management approaches as a support, even an insignificant cause could have a massive effect.

During the process, don't give up when encountering frustration. While trying to develop morality and culture, many people begin to waver in their determination when they encounter disdain and questioning. This isn't right. If you really wish to save this organization, besides generating some interest, what's most important is a brave and fierce heart. Only in this way can abundant fruits ripen.

You often fought in childhood, but now, your words and manner are full of dreamlike gentleness. What's the key factor for such dramatic change?

I did fight a lot when I was young. In middle school, my record was five fights in one day. I was wounded and almost expelled from school.

In elementary school, I also liked to fight. When I visited my old school, I couldn't recall what I had learned there, but only the many places where I had fought. Sometimes it wasn't easy to fight in school, so we would say, "After lunch, let's go to such and such place." And then we would show up on time and start fighting again. The mountains, riverbanks, and so forth were all our fighting arenas. My life in elementary school was like that.

After I started studying Buddhadharma, especially Mahayana Buddhadharma like the *Guide to the Bodhisattva's Way of Life*, I underwent an enormous change. I strongly believe that this comes from the supreme blessing of the Buddhadharma.

This isn't just my experience. It has also happened to many other people in our Buddhist Institute. Once, when I was giving a teaching, I heard a monk ferociously whispering to the monk beside him, "I'm not going to behave like you. If I hadn't learned Mahayana Buddhadharma, I would absolutely beat you up in my old way." He thought I didn't hear it, but I did.

Obviously, this also requires a special connection to Dharma study. Some people find it's the very thing that they're looking for, while some feel nothing special. This was also true at the time of the Buddha. Without a special karmic connection, it's just like the *Ornament of Clear Realization* says, "Although rain descends from the sky, burned seeds aren't able to germinate." Similarly, although Buddhas have appeared in the world, people without karmic connection receive no benefit.

Whether Dharma study can change someone is really determined by one's own karmic connection and virtuous roots.

Lecture at Xi'an Jiaotong University
November 12, 2011

4. Buddhadharma in the Age of Science and Technology

Buddhism isn't mysticism. It's realism. It's not occult fables, but instructions helping us to face emotion, aging, illness, and death positively and optimistically.

Even if you have a first-rate education, as long as you're a human being, you can't escape from birth and death. Besides your knowledge of science, do you have some knowledge of the nature of mind that controls your birth and death? Do you have some knowledge of how to live a good life?

In the 1950s, a nineteen-year-old college student wrote a letter to Einstein asking what man's purpose might be and what path one should follow.

Einstein believed this question was worthwhile, and his answer to it was "satisfaction of the desires and needs of all, as far as this can be achieved, and achievement of harmony and beauty in the human relationships. This presupposes a good deal of conscious thought and of self-education. It is undeniable that the enlightened Greeks and the old Oriental sages had achieved a higher level in this all-important field that what is alive in our schools and universities."[6]

Today many people dedicate themselves to fame and personal gain, thinking very little about life. Thus, they suffer from more and more afflictive emotions. Our rhythm for pursuing material progress is just too fast. Many people say, "Time is money; efficiency is life," but where does this lead them? Putting aside other things, let's just look at our pace of walking. A report from the UK says that we walk 10 percent faster than the pace we had a decade ago. If we continue in this way, we soon won't have any time to rest. Being busy and rushing in such a manner every day hasn't brought us comfort, but rather we have become increasingly unhappy.

Lacking moral guidance, outrageous things happen in the pursuit of material progress, such as toxic baby formula and contaminants in food. When science and technology are in the hands of people who don't believe in the law of karmic cause and effect, in order to satisfy their insatiable desire, they can do whatever heinous things they like.

In particular, for the younger generation, without the blessing and restriction of Buddhist concepts, some, I'm afraid, may go to extremes and even do harm to society.

Albert Einstein wrote, "Science without religion is lame, religion without science is blind." What does this mean? Without the guidance of religion and moral ethics, science creates more harm than benefit for humans, and eventually it will cease to advance. On the other hand, if religion can't withstand the test of science, its theories won't convince people, and practitioners will end up puzzled. This understanding applies just as well today as it did during Einstein's time. If this is correctly understood, it can help to rebalance society.

There's another statement that has been shared widely online: "Human knowledge of science and technology has already conquered outer space, but not the space of the human mind." Indeed, no matter how sophisticated scientific instruments are, they can only help us to observe external objects. When exploring our inner world, there's no other approach than meditation to unveil its mysteries.

Master Tai Xu once said, "The more developed the science, the more obvious the significance of Buddhism." When the truths revealed by the Buddha have been decisively proven, people will be able to discern what they really need for their mind, and Buddhism can bring people the most profound benefits.

I admire practitioners meditating in quiet mountains; they give up a comfortable life, rest in a state of enlightenment, and enjoy inner happiness every day. Though most of us can't adopt this kind of life at present, if we understand some Buddhist teachings such as cultivating an altruistic mind and then apply these in our life, we can give up forms of attachment and not take things to heart no matter what happens. This is also a great accomplishment.

Although I often can't really make a difference in people's lives or substantially benefit them, I take it as a small mission to try anyway. I've studied Buddhism for a long time, and even though my studies were sometimes limited, I've read a great number of sutras and tantras in the traditions of Tibetan, Chinese, and Theravada Buddhism. The more I study, the more I feel the Buddha's wisdom is inconceivable. As a Buddhist, wherever I go, whether it be a metropolis or remote area, I always teach Buddhadharma.

During this process, I feel I'm really just a student. When people call me "teacher" or "Khenpo" I feel ashamed. I don't even think that I'm a qualified student, let alone a teacher. However, Buddhism is so wonderful and people today really need it, so I can't help myself from sharing it. The reason is that I myself have benefited from it and also clearly understand that what I've gained is exactly what modern people need. Therefore, it's absolutely necessary for each of us to understand Buddhist theories, even if just out of curiosity. No matter how times change, Buddhist philosophy can accommodate the needs of every individual and will never become outdated.

Science needs compassion.

The compassion of the Buddha pervades and is innately present within all sentient beings, whether humans or animals.[7] By
nature, humans have innate compassion. Even if you don't believe
in Buddhism, when you see that a sentient being is being cruelly
injured or killed, you naturally have an impulse to intervene. No
matter how advanced science becomes, it's impossible to neglect
compassion.

As a state of mind, however, compassion doesn't emerge in everyone at every moment. Only when we understand why we should
be compassionate and how to cultivate compassion can we develop
genuine compassion and put down animosity calmly.

To this end, we can think of compassion in terms of nonviolence.
Mahatma Gandhi based his values on nonviolence and truth. For us,
nonviolence isn't a political principle, but is the Buddha's instruction for practitioners. The Vinaya says, "When others beat me, I will
not beat back; when others curse me, I will not curse back; when
others hate me, I will not hate them; when others destroy me, I will
not seek revenge." These are principles of nonviolence. Do we need
these? The answer is absolutely. Every corner of this world needs
compassion and nonviolence.

Some people may argue that this is cowardice and that we should
resist when being bullied. In fact, to use violence to curb violence
only escalates matters. From what we have seen, wars bring tremendous harm and little benefit to nations and individuals. Tolerance is
the best solution for dispute. As Gandhi said, "An eye for an eye will
only make the whole world blind."

I heard that several decades ago a khenpo was imprisoned and
mistreated for more than twenty years. After he was released, a great
master asked him, "What were you most afraid of when you were in

prison?" He replied, "I was most afraid of losing compassion toward those who harmed me."

Another great master from Qinghai was also criticized and stigmatized at public meetings every day during those years. Just before these meetings would take place, he always quietly wished, "May the merit of my patience today benefit all sentient beings, including those who beat me." While being attacked, he kept watching his mind for a thought of hatred. After the meetings, he dedicated the merit to those people again, and if time allowed, he recited silently the *Great Vows of the Bodhisattva Samantabhadra*. If he had no time, he recited some short dedication prayers.

He treated tribulation as practice and applied the "three supremes" to it: generating bodhichitta at the beginning, avoiding attachment during the practice, and dedicating virtue at the end. The public criticism and torment facilitated the perfection of his practice.

Unfortunately, nowadays very few people understand or apply this philosophy.

Understanding the Buddha's wisdom is essential.

Buddhism emphasizes wisdom above all, but many people neglect this and their Buddhist practice is artificial, focusing only on praying for safety. This is a shame. While Buddhist practice can certainly bring safety, this isn't its fundamental purpose. Rather than a certificate of taking refuge or attending a Buddhist ceremony, understanding the Buddha's unique wisdom is most fundamental.

It's easy to go astray if we practice without study. Sakya Pandita said, "If one practices blindly without sufficiently listening to the Dharma, he or she will be born as an unwise animal." Therefore, we first have to understand Buddhist theory. For instance, before meditation, we should first understand why we meditate, how to calm the mind, and what will happen after it's calmed. After having this theoretical understanding, then it's okay to meditate.

If study is separated from practice, we can't taste the profound Buddhadharma either. The *Shurangama Sutra* states that without practice, studying a great number of Buddhist teachings is the same as not having studied at all, just as one can't dispel hunger by merely saying the names of different kinds of food without eating any. This is just like people who have never practiced or even reflected on the Dharma but can teach Buddhist sutras brilliantly. Even if they teach the Dharma for their entire life, their habitual tendencies will still remain fixed.

We can't access the Buddha's wisdom without Buddhist scriptures. I highly recommend the *Guide to the Bodhisattva's Way of Life*, by Shantideva, the *Words of My Perfect Teacher*, by Patrul Rinpoché, and the *Great Treatise on the Stages of the Path to Enlightenment*, by Jé Tsongkhapa. The best approach is to study and practice at the same time. In order to realize Buddhadharma, one should study earnestly and practice steadily.

Some people say, "I'm busy with taking care of my family and career now. I don't have time. I'll think about it when I'm old." But when that time comes, your energy and intelligence are failing, and the right causes and conditions may have already disappeared. Great masters have earnestly and repeatedly advised, "Don't wait till old age to start learning about the path, for in tombs are many youth."

Nowadays, it's true that most Buddhists are middle-aged or elderly. Most young people value their present life and think that Buddhism has nothing to do with them. However, in my opinion, even just for securing a better life, Buddhist philosophy is indispensable.

These days I've been discussing Buddhadharma in a number of universities, not for any political or economic purpose, nor with the intention of manipulating anyone with the Dharma. My goal is only to share Buddhist truths with those who don't yet know about them and to help those who are already familiar with Buddhism to understand it more deeply.

Fortunately, many young people are starting to pay attention to Buddhism. Not long ago, we held the first World Youth Buddhist Symposium, and students from different parts of the world attended. Some students shared that they had experienced inconceivable phenomena, some could remember their past lives, some felt the blessings of buddhas and bodhisattvas, and some experienced obvious change after they prayed at difficult times. There were many interesting talks.

To accept Buddhadharma, young people usually go through the following steps: at the beginning, they resist it; in the middle, they're curious but skeptical about it; and finally, they gain benefit from it. If its benefit is genuinely experienced, who would refuse it?

Finally, to wish you well, let me borrow a remark from Elder Monk Xu Yun: "May the field of your mind grow no ignorant grasses but let wisdom flowers blossom everywhere."

Q&A

I'm still skeptical about Buddhadharma. My question is, How did human beings come into being? Who created us? Was it the Buddha?

According to the *Abhidharmakosha*, human beings didn't simply evolve from a common ancestor shared with apes, as is described by the theory of evolution. This text explains that every human being or form of life has to go through a lengthy series of migrations across lifetimes to reach its present state. Human beings weren't created by anybody—not God nor the Buddha—but came into being in accordance with their karma.

Buddha Shakyamuni is the fourth buddha of the one thousand buddhas to appear in this eon of virtue. Before him, three buddhas had already appeared in this human realm. Buddhas appear in this world to turn the wheel of Dharma and liberate sentient beings. This isn't an indication of the beginning of human beings' existence.

What's the Buddhist view on the theory of evolution?
Even if Darwin were still alive, it would be very difficult for him to explain the complexity of the development of life based solely on his theory of evolution. Currently even the scientific community has been questioning his theory. Several years ago, more than five hundred scientists publicly expressed their skepticism about this theory.

According to the theory of evolution, human beings have come into being simply due to random mutation and natural selection. If this were true, then everyone should have a relatively similar degree of suffering and happiness, intelligence, and so on, but this isn't the case. From the Buddhist point of view, putting aside other factors, suffering and happiness arise from previous karma.

When examined carefully, the theory of evolution, in a certain sense, hinders us from understanding the true nature of the complexity of life and establishing the correct outlook on life and its value.

My research isn't going well. I'm really upset. How can Buddha-dharma help me?
Praying to the buddhas is helpful, but will it ensure that all your wishes will come true? Not necessarily. This is because your own karmic causes and conditions also must be taken

into account. Just like when we're sick, some illnesses can be cured and some can't. But do we still go see a doctor? Of course we do. This is also true for praying to the buddhas. When we encounter unfavorable conditions, praying to the buddhas must bring blessings. But how much difference it makes depends on our own faith and merit.

In this increasingly complicated age, how have Tibetan culture and Buddhism been impacted?
Foreign cultures have undeniably had a great impact on Tibetan culture and Buddhism. But so far I don't see any big problems. This is because Tibetan Buddhist culture is mainly preserved in monasteries, and monasteries are usually in remote mountains, not open to the outside. In addition, the lineage holders, many respected geshés and khenpos, still remain in this world. And Tibetan people themselves, whether monastics or laypeople, place great importance on Buddhist study and practice, and view Buddhadharma as the wish-fulfilling jewel, and so don't forsake it easily.

Some Tibetans, after they go to Chinese areas or abroad, love their lives there and end up paying too much attention to their appearance and lifestyle, and so their belief gradually fades away. By contrast, many Western people have begun to value and study Tibetan culture and Buddhism.

In the end, I believe this essential part of the Tibetan people's heritage will return, even if it's from Chinese areas to Western countries and then back to its homeland.

You wrote in one of your books that the quintessence of Buddhism is great compassion and wisdom. If "great compassion" refers to the great compassionate mind, bodhichitta, sympathy, and empathy, then what's wisdom?

In Buddhism, we talk about two kinds of wisdom: one is the intelligence to be able to discern what to adopt and what to reject, as well as to accept what's true. For university students, this intelligence can help you make a living; if you lack this sort of intelligence, you may not even find a job. Such intelligence is acknowledged in Buddhism as a type of wisdom.

However, the second kind of wisdom is the most fundamental and important category of wisdom. This is the wisdom that comprehends the true nature of all phenomena. Different from intellectual understanding, it entails perfect, unsurpassable enlightenment. Such wisdom is the most profound and advanced.

Buddhism talks about karma, the meeting of causes and conditions, so how does karma work?

Buddhism believes that one's suffering and happiness come from the meeting of causes—negative and positive karma—as well as many complicated conditions. The seed you plant (the cause) will determine the fruit that it bears (the effect).

Negative karma is like poisonous seeds that bear poisonous fruits, or suffering. Positive karma is like medicinal seeds that bear wonderful fruits, namely, happiness. Different fruits come from different causes. Various conditions help this process, just as sunshine, water, soil, and so forth help a seed to grow.

For example, siblings have the same parents, but their personality, talents, jobs, and experiences can be very different.

What are the causes of all these differences? The karma carried by each of them from their previous lifetimes

If you want to further your understanding, then study Buddhist scriptures, contemplate this theory, and examine all the phenomena in your life with your understanding of this theory.

I've been educated in materialism since childhood. How should I understand reincarnation?

In the current scientific community, past and future lives aren't completely denied. For example, Professors Ian Stevenson and Jim Tucker in America have collected several thousand cases from across the world that support the existence of past and future lives. Many people don't accept this idea due to the outlook they have acquired over the course of their lives, but as information spreads rapidly and new cases continue to emerge, this phenomenon will attract more and more attention.

In regard to the debate about reincarnation, if there's no convincing evidence to disprove it and a large number of cases to prove it, negative views on it will collapse by themselves.

Apart from cases like those that Stevenson and Tucker describe, there are also specialized theories in Buddhism. To put it simply, due to self-attachment and afflictive emotions, an individual creates karma. When this life cycle ends, the next life cycle will carry this karma and produce another form of life, from which the boundless flow of cyclic existence comes into being. Only when the wisdom of selflessness arises will these cycles be put to an end.

Buddhism isn't simple preaching; you're allowed to analyze such questions by yourself. The best way to analyze them is to debate. In Tibet, we use a formal system of debate to investigate these subjects. Topics like the existence of past and future lives can easily be debated for a couple of months. At the end, if you have no materials to support your hypothesis but I still do, then you lose, and my view is accepted. This is actually a very good method.

In the process of seeking truth, we should have reservations, and then use logic to establish or refute it. I think this is rather scientific.

As a youth, I feel that the four noble truths, the twelve links of dependent origination, and the view of emptiness are very attractive, but every time I read about this buddha and that bodhisattva in a scripture, I feel they're too removed from us and don't really believe in them. So, are they real?
Yes, they're real. Buddha Shakyamuni was indeed in this world 2,500 years ago. However, he wasn't a god. Rather, he simply came to this world to spread the Dharma and introduce the truth to people. His thoughts were written down and called "sutras" afterward. The life of the Buddha isn't myth.

The four noble truths, the twelve links of dependent origination, and the view of emptiness represent the ideology of the Buddha. Throughout the ages, many people have reached enlightenment through study and practice in accordance with these teachings. This can be found in the biographies of many great masters. For ordinary people, their realization is incomparable. If this is true for the Buddha's followers, how can the excellent qualities of the Buddha and bodhisattvas such as Avalokiteshvara and Maitreya not be real? If you study the teachings of the Buddha but at the same time deny the existence of the Buddha, it's contradictory.

Having doubts is understandable. Not knowing enough Dharma and being influenced by popular culture makes it difficult to gain faith in supreme realization. But when studying the Dharma, don't just accept what makes sense to you initially. In the case of unknown knowledge, you can't deny its existence just because you don't understand it.

I've always wished to understand the theory of tathagatagarha (buddha nature) comprehensively. How should I begin?
You can read some of the most fundamental and essential sutras and commentaries, such as the *Tathagatagarbha Sutra*, Maitreya's *Uttaratantra Shastra*, and the *Lion's Roar: A Commentary on Sugatagarbha*, by Mipham Rinpoché, as well as the *Mountain Doctrine*, by the Jonangpa scholar Dolpopa Sherab Gyaltsen.

Detailed elaboration of tathagatagarbha theory can be found in these sutras and in the commentaries of the Sutrayana.

I have a strong interest in Buddhadharma, but you said that interest isn't enough, that one must practice. How should I practice?
You should practice in the appropriate order: first, you can study the *Words of My Perfect Teacher*, also known as *A Guide to the Preliminary Practices of the Great Perfection*, which elaborates practice in great detail.

For example, you can first meditate on the difficulty of obtaining a human body and make sure your current human body is used for the most meaningful goal. Then you can meditate on the impermanence of life and truly understand that death is certain but the time of death is uncertain, and through this you cultivate a sense of urgency to practice diligently. Next, contemplate the infallible law of karmic cause and effect and gain the certainty that after death, you'll take rebirth in higher or lower realms according to your karma, so you must give up nonvirtue and practice virtue. Then think about the defects of samsara. Wherever you're born, whether in the higher or lower realms, it's still suffering and not liberation, so you have to liberate yourself from it.

In this manner, practice step by step and lay a solid foundation. Otherwise, if you start with the most advanced Dharma, though it sounds great, it will be very difficult for you to uproot your afflictive emotions.

In order to eliminate afflictive emotions, let alone attain liberation from samsara, the wisdom of emptiness is indispensable. Such wisdom has to be developed on the foundation mentioned above. Offering incense, making prostrations, and practicing virtuous deeds generates merit, but such practices can't destroy self-attachment, so you still end up drifting in samsara.

A commentary called the *Three Principles of the Path*, by Jé Tsongkhapa, explains three key points for liberation: the mind of renunciation, the awakened mind of bodhichitta, and nondual wisdom. Nondual wisdom is the wisdom of emptiness, which is the most important aspect.

Nowadays, many Buddhists only pay attention to practicing virtues on the surface, but this is far from enough. To reach liberation, studying and practicing pith instructions is necessary.

In Hong Kong, everybody is busy earning money. Life is enjoyable, but we're under stress. How can we work on our afflictive emotions?

This isn't just true in Hong Kong; it's the same in mainland China now. People are increasingly busy, talking on the phone all day long, finding it so difficult to keep quiet even for a moment. Actually, everyone should slow down and think, "What am I doing?" The purpose of life isn't just to earn money. Many people reach the end of their life journey while they're still making money. When looking back in that moment, everything they pursued seems illusory and unreal.

The best way to reduce afflictive emotions is to cultivate contentment. Happiness doesn't come from money. Most people's agony stems from discontentment, not from a lack of money. As the old saying goes, "Contentment brings happiness." This is very wise.

Contentment isn't a passive attitude but a way to stop obsessing. If you have no opportunity to make money, then just accept your circumstances; if you do have the opportunity to make money, then go ahead and make use of that opportunity. However, don't make money only to enjoy it yourself; make money to help those who can't even feed themselves.

If you can adopt such an attitude, you'll live very happily, doing what you like and earning what you can. At the same time, you'll have fewer afflictive emotions.

What does the statement "objects are the work of mind" mean?
"Objects are the work of mind" is the view of the Chittamatra or Mind Only school of Buddhism. It means that all external and internal objects are produced by the mind. Everything is just like a dream; nothing in a dream is real. It's all contrived by the mind. Do "objects" appear? Yes, but they're illusory.

To understand this point further, you can study the *Twenty Verses on Mind Only*, the *Thirty Verses on Mind Only*, the *Shurangama Sutra,* and the *Lankavatara Sutra.* Afterward, you'll understand that "the three realms are just mind; every phenomenon is only mind." Everything appearing to us is just an illusion, but because our mind is obscured by ignorance, we see it as real.

Buddhism says, "Form is emptiness, emptiness is form." If form is empty, then why do we need to have compassion toward an ant, for example? Compassion itself is also empty, so why should we discern virtue and vice?

Emptiness is form but emptiness doesn't mean nothingness. On top of that, all forms still appear.

"Form is emptiness, emptiness is form" is the fundamental idea of the Middle Way view and the quintessence of the *Heart Sutra.*

From the point of view of the nature of reality, which is the realization of the buddhas and bodhisattvas, and at the level of the nature of all phenomena, form and emptiness are inseparable. But at the conventional and phenomenal level, where we currently are, form isn't emptiness and emptiness isn't form. Therefore, we must understand this in two different contexts according to the nature of reality and then phenomenal appearance.

Just like in quantum mechanics, when a vase is examined, it's ultimately composed of particles such as quarks and subquarks, but in its appearance, or when we see it with our eyes, do we see particles? No, we see a vase. Why do our eyes fail to see particles? Because we're talking about two different levels of reality, so don't confuse one with the other.

Regarding an ant, at the ultimate level, yes, its nature is empty. But since we haven't realized emptiness, we still need to cultivate compassion based on its suffering and happiness. Similarly, at the ultimate level, the nature of compassion is also empty, but on the phenomenal level, virtue and vice bring different results, so we still need to give up vice and practice virtue. This law is at the conventional level and anyone living in this world can't be exempted from it.

If you have a comprehensive understanding of Buddhism, you'll find that it's easier to understand this point.

Different sects or schools have different interpretations of Buddhadharma. Have you ever come across some opposition? How did you respond?

Yes, I have, and I think it's good.

If I'm indeed wrong, I won't obstinately cling to my words when you oppose them. I must accept your opposition respectfully. This is a basic tenet in Buddhist training. If you have no sound reasons to support your view, however, I'll confidently insist on my own point of view.

If the discussion of different views escalates to a personal attack, I won't feel upset either. In my opinion, it's a pleasure to exchange ideas with an open mind. But even if there were a personal attack, I wouldn't fear it as long as what I insisted is true.

Besides, an opposition or an attack can be an opportunity to reflect and improve oneself. Galileo said, "See now the power of truth; the same experiment which at first glance seemed to show one thing, when more carefully examined, assures us of the contrary."

Lecture at Hong Kong University of Science and Technology
November 24, 2011

5. STRESS-RELIEVING WISDOM

In order to create more spare time, we invented machines, only to find that we're wearier. In order to communicate better, we invented phones, only to find that we're lonelier. In order to become smarter, we invented the internet, only to find that we're duller. Human beings can guess the beginning but fail to predict the end; what has been neglected here?

TODAY HUMAN MINDS are restless, confused, and complex. As a result, traditional culture and knowledge are necessary. In this time of advanced science and technology, useful knowledge is often stored in computers and smartphones; very little is kept in our brains. We don't bother to memorize valuable information but take snapshots of it and save it. Then when we need it, we can't find it. I heard that once at an international conference, there was a power failure during one famous professor's talk. Because he, like all the others, had prepared everything as a PowerPoint slideshow, he couldn't explain effectively his own research.

Science and technology can bring us many conveniences, but if we rely on them too much, they'll only make us restless. In fact, they have the potential to be dangerous. As we develop science and technology, we must not forsake our traditions.

Today, I'm going to talk about how modern people like us can relieve stress from a Buddhist perspective.

Ancient teachers can help.

Apart from examinations and tuition, students don't have too much stress. But after graduation, all sorts of stress will come.

First there's the pressure of getting a job. Just a job isn't enough, because you want a pleasant job. Once you find one, you have to deal with those above and below you and solve endless interpersonal problems. Next, you have to pay your student loan and mortgage or rent. You probably want to get married and raise children too. In Buddhism, it's said that we should make offerings to the Three Jewels, but worldly people have to "make offerings" to many other objects throughout their life, and they're constantly under pressure and filled with anxiety.

Will all of this stress disappear after you attend a lecture like this one? Of course not. Nonetheless, can a tradition such as Buddhism help you relieve stress? Yes, it can. Although some stress is unavoidable, some of it we create for ourselves. We don't necessarily have to endure such stress. Once you understand this, you'll understand the significance of traditions like Buddhism.

Many young people have a bright and pretty appearance, radiating health and vigor, and are equipped with all sorts of high-tech devices. It seems like they're indestructible. The truth is that when difficulties and problems arise, they falter because they're severely lacking in resilience. This situation can be changed quite easily. Even in the twenty-first century, the best approach involves looking back in time and learning from ancient teachers.

Confucius, one of these ancient teachers, lived around 500 BCE. During his time, civilizations were evolving rapidly. In China, alongside Confucius, a number of philosophers such as Laozi, Mencius, and Xunzi appeared. In the West, there were also many great philosophers, such as Socrates and Plato. In India, Buddha Shakyamuni, the founder of Buddhism, was also born. Written records of their thoughts and opinions have impacted world thought and culture up to the present.

In terms of material affluence and technology, ancient people can't compare to us, but in terms of spirit, the further we progress, the more necessary it is to look back and study ancient thought regarding how to do things and be a good person. Obviously, it's unlikely that you'll be greatly transformed through one lecture or book. However, at least you might view your life from a different angle, and from then on, changes in your life may begin to take place.

Beautiful scenery won't eliminate your stress.

Recently, many spokesmen in China have been claiming that their city is "the city that gives people the strongest feeling of happiness." In reality, if you really lived in one of those cities, you would find the index of happiness there isn't that high. For instance, it has always been said that the natural scenery of Guilin[8] is the best in the world. Outsiders can easily believe that living in such a beautiful place must be a very happy experience. However, residents here may not have any special feeling about this, and the beautiful scenery may do nothing to reduce their stress.

According to some researchers, China is the most stressed out nation in the world today. Not long ago, during the week of the national holiday on October 1, in order to relieve stress, about seven hundred million Chinese people went on vacation. Unfortunately, due to the massive numbers of cars on the road, many people spent most of their time in traffic. When they finally arrived, there was nowhere left to stay. In order to relax, they went on vacation, only to find themselves even more exhausted.

This is what Buddhists mean by the statement "All contaminated phenomena are suffering." Many phenomena appear to cause happiness, but their essence is still suffering, just as many rich and powerful people appear enviable, but only they know their own bitterness.

It's not escapism for Buddhism to emphasize suffering. With earnest contemplation, you'll find that it's in accord with the human mind and is the truth of all phenomena. Even for non-Buddhists, if they approach their life with this in mindset, they'll find much greater comfort and ease. Otherwise, without understanding the truth of suffering, even the small stresses that normally aren't worth mentioning can cause a mental breakdown.

Worldly ways to relieve stress only divert your focus.

Obviously, there are many ways to reduce stress, both worldly and supramundane. What are the worldly means? When under pressure, some people like to talk with an understanding friend or relative. Some choose to find a good book and immerse in it to forget their afflictions. Some prefer to listen to music and hope to dispel their restlessness with the melodies and rhythms. Others decide to forget what's in front of them and take a vacation to divert their focus.

There are also some inappropriate methods, like drowning one's sorrow in liquor or trying to forget worries by gambling or other such behaviors.

These methods can temporarily divert our attention, but the stress isn't actually removed. If the problem isn't solved from its root, unwise behaviors may emerge.

Once there was a university professor who doted on his daughter but at the same time put pressure on her by constantly telling her, "You must win honor for our family." His daughter studied very hard and always ranked among the best from elementary school to high school. However, during twelfth grade, her performance dropped a little. Before the college entrance exams, she looked at her school options. Her grades weren't high enough to gain entrance to one of the top universities, so she thought to go to a university of the second category. Her father set himself against it and said, "As a university professor, isn't it a disgrace for me if my daughter can't go to a top university?" Under such pressure, the daughter became depressed and increasingly quiet. One morning before an examination, the father found his daughter dead in bed; she had killed herself by taking an overdose of sleeping pills. Beside her pillow was a suicide note that read: "Your undutiful daughter is leaving! I really can't meet your expectations. I have no courage to face you. Thank you very much for raising me these past eighteen years ..." We can only imagine how these parents suffer from such an end.

Nowadays, many young people are inclined to commit suicide or self-harm when encountering relationship problems, unfair treatment, or frustrations. This is really unwise. We must understand that our human bodies and this life are very difficult to obtain. If we don't make good use of it and easily give it up, it's indeed the worst choice we can make.

Stress is something that everyone has to face. There's no way to escape it. Rather, we need to find the correct methods to deal with it. Young people in particular encounter many problems that aren't easy to endure. At those times, it's important to understand how to adjust the mind. Otherwise, if the mind isn't under control, they may end up suffering from depression. Even if they're not mentally ill, they may act out in ways that bring suffering not only to them but also to everyone around them.

Stress can also motivate us.

Stress isn't necessarily a bad thing. We need some stress; otherwise we may just muddle through this life without achieving anything. Some have said that 25 percent of human potential and intelligence is developed by effort, while 75 percent is unlocked by stress.

Just as some teachers wouldn't have read so many books if they didn't need to give lectures, similarly, students wouldn't necessarily study so earnestly without the stress of examinations and employment. The proper amount of stress is very helpful.

For wise people, the greater the stress, the greater the achievement. This is called the "bouncing ball effect" in psychology. The stronger the force a ball receives, the higher it can bounce. I have taken this theory very personally.

Why do I often leave my monastery to give lectures? If I'm not willing to teach, nobody can force me to do it. However, I always think that meeting people from a variety of backgrounds allows me to learn more. For me, a little bit of stress can keep me from divorcing myself from this time.

Therefore, it's necessary to develop oneself under stress. Life is like a nail, which won't voluntarily enter a wall without being hammered. Similarly, without stress, our potential wisdom can't be utilized.

Within limits, stress can be transformed into motivation. It's like the air inside the balloon: the more there is, the bigger the balloon. However, just as the capacity of a balloon has a limit, so does the endurance of humans. Once the limit is exceeded, the balloon bursts and the humans collapse.

If we were like a fallen tree, we would just lie on the ground until we rotted away. As humans, however, even if we fall down, we can stand up again. We can develop a strong mind to prevent stress from overwhelming us.

A piece of information may be helpful to add here: Psychologist Kelly McGonigal from Stanford University suggests that stress may only be bad for us if we believe it's negative, so she urges us to see stress in a positive way instead of as an enemy.

Buddhism can help with stress.

When Buddhism is mentioned, some people associate it with superstition. For instance, some people believe that Buddhism is non-scientific because it acknowledges past and future lives, as well as the law of karmic cause and effect. This is a misunderstanding. Each of you has the ability to think critically, so you can scrutinize with your own intelligence whether Buddhism makes sense.

As far as I know, Buddhist theories like these haven't been disproven by science. Take reincarnation, for example. Buddhism states that the good merit of this life partially comes from the accumulation of merit in past lives and partially is acquired through effort in the present life. From this "cause" of past lives that ripens into the "effect" in the present life, we can extrapolate the existence of past and future lives. I always talk about this topic, and many people are completely confused by it. Although I don't have the clairvoyance to directly perceive it, thanks to reasoning and various reported cases, I find it impossible to refute the existence of past and future lives.

Modern science has a roughly six-hundred-year history. On the topic of reincarnation, this history falls into two phases. In the first phase, scientists didn't explicitly deny reincarnation. In the second phase, due to the popularity of certain ideologies, some scientists began to argue against this idea. However, toward the end of the twentieth century, a number of scientists began to change their position, and through studies in medical science, psychology, and quantum mechanics, they have found that the idea that nothing is left after death is false.

For example, Sir John Carew Eccles, one of the Nobel Prize winners in medicine in 1963, writes that within a human body, there is consciousness that is free from shape or color. It can control our brains just as we control a computer. When our brains are dead, this consciousness or self is immortal. Through his research, he came to the conclusion that after we die, we don't completely cease to be like the extinguishing of a candle or the drying up of a river.

Even the most notable names of science didn't take a finite view of our existence. For example, Newton, the founder of modern science, admitted the possibility of future lives. Einstein also had great interest in Buddhist theories in his later years. A few days ago, an overseas Buddhist friend sent me a couple of books. One of them mentioned that in his later years, Einstein talked about the good qualities of Buddha Shakyamuni and how the Buddha viewed this world.

Some of the people who deny the existence of past and future lives know neither traditional culture nor modern science. They believe that human beings came to be in this world by accident and that after being born, we'll die and that's it—there's nothing left. According to their logic, everything, including all the stress and suffering that we encounter in this life, has no karmic causes or conditions.

The majority of these people believe that human consciousness is generated by the brain, but this hasn't been validated by science, and many Nobel laureates don't accept this idea. Rather, experiments have found that even without brains, some human beings, chickens, and other animals can still have feelings, consciousness, and mental activities. Therefore, consciousness can exist outside of the brain.

It's necessary for people who reject the existence of past and future lives to study early philosophy, especially treatises by ancient Greek philosophers. Even some of the earliest Christians believed in reincarnation. In Confucianism, the existence of past and future lives isn't emphasized, but we can still find written record of it.

Accepting the law of karmic cause and effect can spare us a lot of stress.

After understanding the existence of past and future lives, we can then accept the fact that everything runs in accord with the law of karmic cause and effect and stop insisting on something that doesn't have a cause to support its happening. The Buddhist view is that when conditions come together, phenomena arise, while when conditions fall apart, phenomena cease. When causes and conditions are present for something, it takes place regardless; when causes and conditions are missing, there's no remedy in any case. If we understand this point, we can save ourselves a lot of suffering.

When in love, some young people ignore karmic causes and conditions and blindly chase after their desire. The result is that the stronger their attachment, the faster they lose their loved one. Just like grasping sand, the tighter you hold it, the faster it leaks away. When facing problems, if we know that everything results from a previous karmic cause, we'll have an attitude and techniques completely different from those who have no idea of this concept.

Most of what you learned in school won't necessarily be used later in your life. According to some statistics, we use only about 15 percent of what we have learned. Learning how to adjust your mind can't be found in your textbooks, but this is the most fundamental and requisite knowledge. Young people in particular need to learn this. If you can master this, you'll eliminate a lot of stress and even the root cause of stress. The effect of this approach is incomparable to other methods, like reading books or listening to music.

To reduce stress, be content.

Today many people like to compete with others, and most of what they're pursuing isn't what they really need. Competition and vanity lead to excessive demand. For instance, simple houses and cars are enough for most people, but the majority believe that the more expensive, the better. In order to satisfy their vanity, they create immense pressure for themselves.

Compared with them, farmers are perhaps happier. Although their material conditions aren't as good as urbanites, their pressure isn't as great as theirs either. Some urbanites live in mansions, drive luxurious cars, and wear name-brand clothes, but they feel insecure and aren't necessarily happier.

Of course, the definition of happiness also differs with time.

Once, Mo Yan, the 2011 Nobel Prize in Literature laureate, was asked about his motivation for writing. Mo Yan answered that decades ago it was said that a writer in Jinan lived such a "corrupt" life that he would eat three meals of dumplings in one day. That was China in 1957, when most people couldn't have even one meal of dumplings per year. So, Mo Yan thought, "What a happy life it is to be a writer! If I can write novels, maybe I could also have three meals of dumplings in one day." This was the cause of his career as a writer and his understanding of happiness during that time.

When material goods are in short supply, people feel the best thing is to be able to eat whatever they like at any time. However, the happiness brought by material goods fades away and even disappears once it's finished. Such happiness is relative and inconstant.

When I visited America in 1993, more than half of all Americans owned a car, so they could drive themselves to wherever they needed. I first thought they were very happy. Later, when I was talking with some rich people, I found out they were unhappy because they couldn't afford their own airplanes!

The better the living conditions, the greater the expectations people set for themselves. Consequently, their stress is greater. For some people, the only time that they'll finally let go of all their desires is on their deathbeds.

To diminish suffering, the first step is to let go.

In order to suffer less in life, the first step is letting go. Only by doing so can stress lessen. If you can go further and cultivate a mind of renunciation, then it's not hard to reach self-liberation.

Obviously, in Buddhism, letting go doesn't mean doing nothing. Rather, it teaches you to give up excessive attachment.

A fable says that once a fox saw grapes in a yard and wanted to have a feast. However, he couldn't get through the fence because he was too fat. So, he gave up eating for three days and three nights and finally entered the yard. After eating his fill, he couldn't get out because of his big stomach. So, he had to repeat the strategy of giving up eating for three days and three nights. Finally, when he got out of the yard, his belly was the same as when he had entered.

Aren't we human beings the same? We come to this world naked and proceed to the next life empty-handed. People put so much effort into acquiring fame and personal gain, but they won't be able to take it with them into the next life.

Instead, learn to let go and have an attitude of letting things happen. Think, "If I make it, I'm lucky, but if I fail, I have at least done my best." If you get what you like, feel happy and grateful, but if you can't get it, it's either beyond your ability or impossible due to your previous negative karma. A result must come from a corresponding cause, so there's no need to grieve when our best effort falls short.

We create our own stress.

A college student set fairly high expectations for himself. His idea was that after graduation, he must find a job in one of the world's top five hundred companies with an annual salary of at least one hundred thousand yuan. In three years, he must have some achievement in his career; in another three years, he must buy a fancy car. He used a lot of "musts" for his dreams. However, after his graduation, he couldn't find a single job that met his criteria. A friend advised him, "Don't set your goal too high. Start with a twenty-thousand-yuan salary. When you have some experience, you'll be paid better." Reality showed him the gap between dreams and facts. Unless we develop an ability to let go, within this gap we'll find great pressure.

Stress is pervasive in this life. Due to the pressures of studying, students wish to graduate quickly, but when they step into society after graduation, stress from jobs, relationships, and life emerge one after another. Then they begin to reminisce about their life in school. Their perspective changes and different stresses rise and fall. This really illustrates the Buddhist view that life is full of suffering.

Relieve stress by helping others.

The phrase "finding joy in helping others" precisely expresses another method for helping others. Researchers at McGill University in Canada also found that through helping others, people can experience a dramatic decrease in their own suffering.

Some people may argue, "I have no money, how can I help others?" Money isn't necessary for helping others. We can help others with kind words showing concern and care or even with facial expressions to encourage them.

A 2009 bestseller in the United States was called *29 Gifts: How a*

Month of Giving Can Change Your Life. The book tells the story of a woman who due to long-term work pressure suffered from a chronic neurological condition. Later, from an African medicine woman, she received an unusual prescription: give to others for twenty-nine days. As she was bedridden, she found this difficult to do, but the medicine woman told her that you don't have to give material gifts— giving others kind words to show your concern and care also counts. With nothing to lose, she tried her best to do this every day. As you must have guessed, she gradually recovered.

When you're not solely concerned about your own interests, your pressure and suffering naturally decrease.

The greatest human suffering comes from selfishness.

Some people really like to cry, but how many tears do they shed out of compassion for others? Was it for the starving children in parts of Africa? Or for the victims of a hurricane? Not likely. Most people cry for this "I"—because someone treated this "I" unkindly, unfairly. When "I" is always put before everything else, suffering is unavoidable.

Buddhism cherishes the compassionate mind of selflessness to the utmost extent. Such a mind is essential for people no matter where they live in the world. Many ideas only remain relevant for a while, but there's a concept that will never fade with time: compassion. Compassion is mankind's greatest treasure. Without compassion, a person will be distanced in any era and in any community. With compassion, not only can this person benefit others, but at a minimum he or she will experience less stress. For instance, when you don't feel well either physically or mentally, but you're busy helping others, you'll naturally forget your own afflictions or pain.

Another way to reduce stress is to cultivate an understanding of emptiness and the wisdom of selflessness. Buddhism teaches that all phenomena are empty of inherent nature. Through comparing this emptiness with quantum mechanics, some modern physicists have concluded that this principle taught by the Buddha 2,500 years ago corresponds to their theories as well. Obviously this doesn't mean that the ultimate nature of materials discovered in quantum mechanics is completely the same as the emptiness in Buddhism. In fact, physicists have only studied the theory of emptiness partially, not fully. However, for those who accept only the sciences, this comparison may help them to find a gateway toward accepting Buddhadharma.

It can be really helpful to reduce stress when one genuinely understands the theory of emptiness. By scrutinizing and analyzing something with wisdom, we'll find that everything—whether it's status, fame, or wealth—is illusory without exception. Even "I" doesn't intrinsically exist. All phenomena are just like empty space. With such a state of mind, how can stress exist? And so suffering evaporates.

In the West and even Japan, more and more people are choosing to practice Buddhism to relieve stress. Their practices fall into two categories. One is through studying the theory of emptiness to understand that all phenomena are unreal, like the virtual world in the film *The Matrix*. The other is through meditation to settle the mind. These are very effective ways to rid suffering from the mind.

Meditation realigns the mind and body.

Many people often feel exhausted both mentally and physically. In such cases, meditation can help adjust their mind and body.

Every day we can take some time to meditate in the morning or at night. Or, every year, we can take a few days off to join a meditation retreat. Many universities have their own meditation society that helps students to improve themselves through meditation. If you understand how to tame your mind, it won't just make your body and mind more pleasant and peaceful, but will also bring joy to the people around you.

Let me introduce two methods of meditation.

The first is meditating with an object. This involves visualizing a Buddha statue or image.

Place a Buddha Shakyamuni image or statue in front of you. Keep your back straight and place your two hands in the position of Buddha Shakyamuni or in the mudra of meditative stability, and then gaze attentively at the body of the Buddha. After a while, close your eyes and visualize the same Buddha statue or image. When the figure becomes blurry or when the mind is distracted, open your eyes to look at the statue or image again, and then close your eyes again to visualize. If you practice in this way for three or four days, the restless mind will gradually transform.

The second method is meditating without objects.

When you're suffering, observe the nature of this suffering at that very moment and look for its whereabouts: is it from the mind or the body? If it's inside the body, in which part of the body does it reside? Finally, having found neither the mind nor the suffering, you abide in this state. Through regular practice like this, a healthy state of mind can be recovered.

It's crucial for modern people to tame their mind. With a healthy state of mind, you won't suffer, experience a breakdown, or agonize, no matter what kind of stress emerges.

When the mind is calm, great ideas will arise naturally.

All people wish to succeed. If they understand Buddhadharma, their potential for success will increase significantly.

Steve Jobs was a faithful Buddhist. Once a Japanese Zen Master told him a story: In ancient times, two monks were debating whether the movement of a streamer was from the wind or from the streamer. One monk said it was the wind that was moving; the other said it was the streamer. After hearing their argument, the Great Sixth Patriarch said it was neither the wind nor the streamer that was moving—what was moving was mind.

Without basic Buddhist knowledge, it would be hard to understand this statement. The Sixth Patriarch was pointing out the profound theory that every phenomenon is the work of the mind. To put it simply, when you dislike a person, no matter what he does, you feel irritated, but when you have a good impression of him, everything he does pleases you. Moreover, when you're anxious, you won't be moved by the beautiful scenery of a place like Guilin. When you're in a great mood, however, you may praise even a scrap heap as beautiful. Thus, there are no absolute good or bad objects—only positive or negative impressions of them.

The Zen master's remarks helped Jobs to understand that everything is created by our mind. From then on, when making an important decision, he tried to use a meditative mind. We see his many ingenious ideas in how he created the Apple empire.

Konosuke Matsushita, the founder of Panasonic and "the God of Management" in Japan, was also a Buddhist. When interviewed at the age of ninety-five, he explained that people with his same talent are everywhere in the world, but the reason for his success was mainly because of his understanding of meditation.

A Japanese Zen master summarized his statement in two remarks:

"Without understanding the meaning of Zen, life is tasteless; without mastering the secret of Zen, an enterprise is hopeless." This means that we must integrate the wonderful taste of meditation into our life. Otherwise, our life will be plagued by busyness, blindness, and depression. Likewise, if we can master the wisdom in Zen and adjust our mind through it, we're likely to achieve great success in our careers.

I hope these ideas can help you relieve your stress and suffering and attain genuine happiness.

Q&A

Every culture needs to change with time in order to adapt to the current era. In the twenty-first century, what changes are needed in Buddhism?

Buddhism has a history of over 2,500 years. I believe its essential wisdom doesn't need to be revolutionized or modernized. This is because Buddhadharma is the essence of human thought. I'm not praising it just because I'm a Buddhist. Buddhism has been evaluated by learned people in the West and East, including the likes of Carl Jung and Lu Xun.[9] Moreover, there are so many great masters who have proven the authenticity of Buddhadharma through their own personal realization.

The format of propagating the Dharma, however, can be changed. For example, Chinese Buddhism developed after Buddhism had integrated with Chinese culture. When it spread in Tibet and integrated with Tibetan culture, Tibetan Buddhism came into being. These are legitimate forms of Buddhism that arose from the causes and conditions of specific times. Nonetheless, the essential wisdom of

Buddhism can withstand the examination of history at any point in time and by any learned person.

What's the essential value of Buddhadharma?
Buddhism can be categorized into the Great Vehicle and the Basic Vehicle. The essential value of the Basic Vehicle is to pursue liberation from one's own afflictive emotions. For the Great Vehicle, self-liberation isn't the main point; its essential value is to benefit others. Seeking Buddhahood is the goal of both vehicles, but the purpose of this goal for the Basic Vehicle is to free one's own self from suffering, while for the Great Vehicle, it's to benefit all sentient beings.

Modern society lacks the spirit of altruism that's found in the Great Vehicle. Whether you advocate for this with the ideas of Marxism, socialism, or Buddhism, the point is that everyone needs to reduce selfishness and increase altruism. Only in this way can our society be in genuine harmony. Therefore, Buddhism isn't out of sync with contemporary times. In fact, it's necessary for our time.

Can you summarize the essence of Buddhism in three to five words?
Afflictive emotions are awakened mind.

When I visited Songzanlin Monastery in Yunnan, I saw a store selling barbecue sausage right beside a shrine room selling incense. Buddhism advocates a vegetarian diet, but the monks there didn't stop them. Does this desecrate the Buddha?
When I visited Potala Mountain, I saw a restaurant called "Buddha's Rays Spreading Pervasively." But when I entered it, they were killing fish. What do you think?

If it wasn't a monastery but in public, I guess there's no choice because not everyone believes in Buddhism.
It wasn't in public; it was right in front of the front door of the monastery.

Do you mean we need to discipline ourselves?
Correct. Understand that around the pure monastery there might be some impure things happening.

Modern society is complex. Things happen that aren't in accord with the intentions of the monastery. People take advantage of the monasteries to earn money. This situation is becoming increasingly common and not only in Yunnan. Nowadays, this problem and many other unfortunate situations also have arisen at the Four Buddhist Holy Mountains of China. Whether the Buddhist community knows about this or not, they can't easily remedy the situation.

Take the example of selling admission tickets. This should never have been applied to monasteries. Unfortunately, due to certain historical reasons, this tradition has formed in China. This isn't common in other countries, and many Buddhists are now demanding a separation of commerce and religion, so as to counter such inappropriate situations. At Larung Gar, we forbid people from taking financial advantage of our presence.

Just now you said, "afflictive emotions are awakened mind." My questions are: What is awakened mind? Where does it come from? What does it indicate?
I'm teaching the Sixth Patriarch's *Platform Sutra* this year, so I've explained this in great detail. Regarding the essence and origin of the awakened mind as well as the methods of

transforming afflictive emotions into the path, if you want to gain real understanding, systematic study is required.

I noticed that the rituals in Tibetan Buddhism aren't only more numerous than but also more canonical than in Chinese Buddhism. The Buddha states in the Diamond Sutra, "There are no conceptual constructions of self, person, sentient beings, or lifespan" and "You should know that what I have taught is just like a raft. If this Dharma should be abandoned, how much more non-Dharma?" My question is, Can we say rituals are also a kind of conceptual construction? If there are too many rituals, does it contradict the spirit of not clinging to such constructions? The Buddha's teaching wasn't targeting only one kind of sentient being or one state of realization.

Some people don't have enough understanding of the Buddhadharma. When they read one or two lines in the *Diamond Sutra* or *Heart Sutra*, they quote it out of context and refute other doctrines of Buddhism. This is obviously unreasonable.

"There are no conceptual constructions of self, person, sentient beings, or lifespan" refers to the nature of ultimate reality, but at the conventional phenomenal level, rituals are indispensable. In fact, like Tibetan Buddhism, Chinese Buddhism and Theravada Buddhism also have many rituals. For instance, in Chinese areas, monasteries have their morning and evening chanting rituals, and monastics have their rituals for receiving precepts as fully ordained monks or nuns.

Rituals are conceptual constructions by nature, but until practitioners reach a high level of realization, they shouldn't be abandoned. This is a fairly simple principle, just like eating. Eating is ultimately a conceptual construction, but until you can survive without eating, you can't simply quit eating.

I often see people make wishes in front of buddha statues in monasteries. What's your opinion of this?
If we make wishes, it's better to do so for sentient beings, not just for one's own career or family. Of course, if this kind of attitude is too hard to cultivate, it's okay to make wishes for oneself. As long as your mind is pure, through the blessings of the buddhas, your wishes will come true relatively easily.

I've read Dharma books for many years, but I feel I'm stupid and unlucky. How can I change my fate?
It's believed in Buddhism that as long as causes and conditions come together, fate is changeable.

If you want to change your fate, read the *Four Lessons of Liao Fan,*[10] always have virtuous thoughts, and do virtuous deeds. Then with time, your fate will improve.

If your past negative karma is too heavy, it's difficult to change your fate immediately, just as when a prisoner is already imprisoned, it's unrealistic to set him free right away. However, no matter what, don't feel hopeless about your life or yourself.

My mother is a Buddhist. She's very confused. When she sees friends or relatives behaving in a manner contradicting the Dharma, she tries to dissuade them. If they don't change, she criticizes them harshly, which makes them angry. If she still can't stop them, she feels restless and it weighs on her conscience. Do you have any suggestions to help her?

As Mahayana Buddhists, we do have the responsibility to benefit sentient beings. However, if the result isn't ideal after we make an effort, we can treat the situation with a mind accepting of the conditions. One of my favorite quotes is "Success and failure are dependent on conditions; our mind has no increase or decrease." We need to be able to let go of anything. There's no need to become elated or deflated or stuck over small things. You can guide your mother with this principle.

We live in a restless age, so I want to calm my mind through meditation in the future. Besides visualizing Buddha statues or images, do you have any better suggestions?
If you want to meditate, you don't have to wait for a future time.

It's not easy to have virtuous thoughts. Once they arise, seize the opportunity. Meditate in your daily life and live your life in meditation.

Some people believe that they have to wait for a specific time to meditate or to engage in charitable activities. They think: "I'll meditate during next year's holidays," or "I'll study the Dharma after I retire." If you keep postponing, you may not have the chance later on.

The Buddha said all sentient beings are equal, but there are so many situations of inequality in this world. How does Buddhism respond to this?
In Buddhism, equality doesn't simply mean everything is exactly the same—the same height, the same skin color. Equality in Buddhism mainly refers to the view that the nature of sentient beings is equal because they all have bud-

dha nature and the cause to become a buddha. Also, the feelings of all sentient beings are equal because we all wish for happiness and dislike suffering. So, we should be compassionate toward every living being.

Such a view of equality isn't valued enough among people today. Many people are only concerned about themselves and neglect the welfare or suffering of sentient beings, and so they never experience genuine happiness.

How can we keep calm when facing inequality?
Think that this is what I have to experience due to the misdeeds I committed in previous lives, or that it's because my merit, wisdom, and ability aren't yet advanced enough. Never shift the blame to others. Rather, treat everything and everyone with gratitude.

Lecture at Guangxi Normal University
November 2, 2012

6. Altruism in Buddhism

*The reason one studies the Dharma is to reach Buddhahood;
the reason to reach Buddhahood is to benefit others, not for
one's own happiness.*

SOME PEOPLE BELIEVE that the Buddha was a mythological figure. This is incorrect. The Buddha did appear in history and is an
admirable historical figure. His life story can withstand any academic
investigation.

Recently, the tooth relic of the Buddha was invited to Burma.
There was a grand ceremony: the vice prime minister along with a
retinue of over two thousand people went to receive it at the airport;
the president and over six thousand government officials saluted
where it was enshrined. During the forty-eight days of its display, a
continuous flow of visitors came to pay homage.

When the finger relic of the Buddha was invited to be revered
in Taiwan, it was also unprecedentedly spectacular. Each day, the
number of visitors exceeded one hundred thousand, and in as few as
eleven days, the total visitors exceeded one million.

Now in the twenty-first century, when people are so fully educated in the ability to distinguish the truth from the false that it's
unlikely for them to blindly believe in anything, why would so many
people revere merely a piece of the remains of the Buddha? So many
other famous people have emerged in the course of human history,

but how many of them have been respected in such a way even after 2,500 years? The pope gets far more visitors, but only while he's alive.

For example, before his death, Einstein requested people not to build a tomb for him, but to scatter his cremated remains at some unknown place. However, for research purposes, the American doctor Thomas Harvey secretly took out his brain and only returned it to the hospital at Princeton University where Einstein passed away forty-two years later. Although a great number of people were infatuated with this brain, it hasn't been revered by people in the same way that relics of the Buddha have, nor does it have their blessing power.

It's probably because I'm a Buddhist that I have a special affection for the Buddha. Nonetheless, you can also investigate this matter in this way: What are the transcendental merits that the Buddha has when compared to other historic famous figures? Why do later generations pay unsurpassable homage to him? What on earth did the Buddha teach in the eighty-four thousand teachings and the vast canonical literature that has helped countless people for millennia?

Some of you may believe in Buddhism, some may not. However, even if you don't, you can still try to learn about it because Buddha-dharma is a subject of wisdom, not mere belief.

Bodhichitta is the quickest path to happiness.

Due to various historical reasons, traditional culture has been severely damaged in China, and this generation is the first to bear the brunt of it. So many people take pursuing wealth, status, and love as their life's goals, and rarely pay attention to morality. Some people even believe that the more merciless they are, the more successful they'll be. Driven by desire, they unscrupulously harm the public for their own benefit.

Behaving in this way can only bring misery. These people don't want suffering, but suffering will visit them again and again. They wish for happiness, but they themselves are destroying their own happiness as if annihilating their enemies.

Pursuing happiness is a part of human nature, but if our approach is wrong, the result will contradict our aims.

The Buddha taught a long time ago that the quick method of obtaining happiness is to benefit others. The upgrade to this method is to cultivate bodhichitta—the awakened mind. The *Mahayana Sutra Requested by Viradatta* states, "The benefit of bodhichitta is that it's the supreme and wonderful medicine that can cure all diseases and bring happiness and peace to all sentient beings."

What is bodhichitta? Ultimately, it's a mind that wishes all sentient beings to be free from suffering, obtain happiness, and reach Buddhahood. This is the most superior virtuous mind, and it's very difficult to cultivate. Without cultivating bodhichitta, even people who have studied the Buddhadharma for their entire life will not be able to wish their enemies happiness, let alone actually help them achieve it.

Bodhichitta is the root of Mahayana Buddhism. It's very hard to understand Mahayana Buddhism without it. Some Buddhists talk a lot about bodhichitta, but they can't even explain its literal meaning. Instead, they confuse it with compassion, virtuous mind, or even charity. This is indeed a shame.

There are two kinds of bodhichitta: aspiration bodhichitta and action bodhichitta. Aspiration bodhichitta is the wish to seek unsurpassable buddhahood to benefit all sentient beings. On the basis of this, action bodhichitta is to take action to fulfill this wish and practice the six perfections and ten thousand deeds.

The *Nirvana Sutra* says, "If someone practices bodhichitta for even one instant, his or her merit can't even be measured by the Buddha."

Of course, not everyone can reach this state right away, so it's good to start by cultivating loving-kindness and compassion. Loving-kindness involves wishing that sentient beings obtain happiness, and compassion involves wishing that sentient beings be free from suffering.

Nowadays, many universities around the world have added cultivating the mind of loving-kindness and compassion to their curricula. In one university, a professor had students meditate on loving-kindness and compassion for ten minutes every morning and afternoon. After two weeks, these students were examined and the data showed that their minds had become gentler and tamer. Even bad-tempered people became more lighthearted. They called this training "ease therapy."

Bodhichitta is the swiftest path to liberation.

I was greatly inspired by a story about the benefit of bodhichitta:

In the eleventh century, there was a great *pandita*, or scholar, named Venerable Atisha. He was born as the crown prince of a region in eastern Bangladesh. One night, Tara appeared in his dream and told him, "You have been a pandita for five hundred lifetimes. It's your mission to liberate sentient beings from the ocean of cyclic existence. Don't leave your mission unfinished!" After waking up, he recalled the aspiration he had made in previous lives and left the palace. Having renounced worldly life, he became a monk, relied on Venerable Rahula as his teacher, and quickly mastered the canonical literature under his teacher's guidance.

One day when he was reading, a question suddenly occurred to him: "What's the swiftest path leading directly to enlightenment? If I follow the Mahayana bodhisattva path, I must liberate others for countless eons to reach the other shore of nirvana. When will I become enlightened?"

He went to ask his teacher this question. His teacher told him: "You're too concerned with your own accomplishment. Cultivate bodhichitta, forget your own benefit, and be concerned with the welfare of others. This is the only path to liberation. Self-attachment is the root of suffering."

Shortly thereafter when he was circumambulating Bodhgaya—the place where the historical Buddha attained enlightenment—he overheard two beautiful women in conversation. One asked, "What's the best way to reach enlightenment?" The other answered, "Selfless bodhichitta is the great path to buddhahood."

The second day, when circumambulating the Buddha stupa and the bodhi tree of enlightenment, he heard an old homeless woman telling a leper, "Bodhichitta is the best way to cross the ocean of suffering and attain enlightenment. Put yourself in others' shoes and give up any selfish thoughts."

After hearing this, he thought, "Everyone here, from the most noble to the most humble, knows the best way to reach enlightenment. And their answer is the same as my teacher's, only I'm still hesitating and doubting."

The third day, when circumambulating the holy temple with prayer beads in his hand, he saw a little bird resting on the knee of the statue of the bodhisattva Avalokiteshvara. The statue said, "To have the bodhichitta of giving up oneself and loving and protecting others is the best path to perfect enlightenment." At that moment, all his doubts disappeared without a trace.

After understanding the importance of bodhichitta, Venerable Atisha went to Indonesia to rely on Master Serlingpa. For twelve years he focused on practicing bodhichitta alone and finally achieved enlightenment.

Sometime later, King Yeshe Ö of Tibet sent several groups of people to India to invite Venerable Atisha to restore the Dharma in Tibet after the suppression of Buddhism by Langdarma.[11] When Venerable Atisha asked Tara to give advice, Tara told him, "If you go to Tibet, countless sentient beings will be benefited by you. However, your lifespan will be reduced by twenty years. You could have lived to be ninety-two years old." Because he'd be able to benefit countless sentient beings, without hesitation, Venerable Atisha went to Tibet to spread the Dharma and restore Tibetan Buddhism. He founded the Kadampa schools and composed *The Lamp for the Path to Enlightenment*; the well-known *Great Treatise on the Stages of the Path to Enlightenment*, by Tsongkhapa, is a commentary based on this work. Eventually, he entered final nirvana at age seventy-two just as predicted, but he was honored as the patriarch who restored Tibetan Buddhism.

Venerable Atisha's method for practicing bodhichitta has been perfectly preserved in Tibet from teacher to disciple right to the present day. The complete instruction and the stages of the specific practice have been widely spread not only in monasteries, but among common people as well. It's mainly due to his contribution that Tibetan Buddhism has developed so much more material on the practice of bodhichitta compared with Chinese Buddhism.

Nowadays, many scholars around the world are very interested in instructions on bodhichitta. However, pure theoretical study isn't enough; without actual practice, its effect can't be fully comprehended. Therefore, the related instructions must be put into practice, and before every action, we must consider whether it will benefit others.

Many people spend most of their time thinking only of themselves. Doing something meaningful for public welfare never occurs to them. Of course, it's unrealistic for ordinary people to completely ignore themselves, but surprisingly often the more you think about yourself, the less you gain, while the more you think about others, the more merit and fortune come to you.

In recent years, I've heard about incidents that demonstrate modern moral degeneration. The reason for this is that we lack an altruistic mind. In Tibet, if a person is hit by a car, every other driver will immediately stop the car and try to save the victim at all costs. Even yaks receive help; Tibetans often go out of their way to help these animals and they even recite prayers for them. It's impossible for many Tibetans to turn a blind eye to other sentient beings' suffering.

In Tibet, there was a well-known great adept named Patrul Rinpoché. Once, when walking to Sershul for a Dharma gathering, he met a widow with her three children walking with great difficulty to the same venue. When he saw their plight, he joined them, carrying the children on his back. Sometimes he even went to beg for food to share with them. He walked with them until they reached their destination.

If we were to encounter such a situation, would we lend a hand like he did?

Most people feel beholden or duty-bound to help their relatives or friends. But in the case of strangers, they think it's not their business. This is a manifestation of our lack of an altruistic mind.

Bodhichitta is a worthy aim.

The core of Buddhism is to benefit others and pray for all sentient beings to be free from suffering and obtain happiness.

Some people may argue, "This mission is impossible, so I don't see it as a very worthy aim."

Let's leave aside whether you can make this happen or not. It's said that when this altruistic mind arises, if the merit were to have shape and form, it couldn't be contained within all of space. *The Great Jewel Heap Sutra* states, "If the merit of bodhichitta had form and orientation, it would occupy all of space and go beyond its capacity."

Carefully savor the words in this quote. It was radiated from the wisdom of the Buddha. It's concise, yet profound. But sadly, most people will never completely realize its meaning.

Some people may also ask, "If Buddhism is really as great as you say, why are there so many people who don't believe in it?"

In fact, any profound knowledge, whether it's sophisticated science and technology or Buddhist theories, can only be deeply understood by very few people. Just as there are very few qualified gem experts who can determine whether a gem is superior or inferior, there are very few people who can distinguish whether a view is authentic wisdom or not.

Nevertheless, whether you understand Buddhism or not, as human beings, we can't avoid misfortune or troubles. If we're proficient at Mahayana mind-training methods, we can immediately remove tremendous suffering in this life, not to mention suffering in future lives. Mind-training methods include meditating on equality of self and other, the exchange of self and other, viewing one's self as less important than others, Venerable Atisha's teachings on recognizing your mother by recalling and repaying her kindness, and so forth.

Some people may also say, "It's enough to know a little bit about Buddhism. Never dive into it too deeply! Otherwise, you'll renounce mundane life and become a monastic."

Such worries are obviously groundless. Everyone has a different disposition; not everyone will become a monastic. In the history of Buddhism, even in the time of Buddha Shakyamuni, the majority of Buddhists were householders, and only a very small number were monastics. In fact, there are a great number of sutras taught by the Buddha for householders.

Bodhisattvas are warriors.

As human beings, whether we believe in Buddhism or not, at least we can understand the preciousness of altruism.

I guess you've heard the Chinese word *pu sa*. It's short for the Sanskrit *bodhisattva*, which means "brave heart." Why are bodhisattvas brave? It takes real bravery to put aside oneself and overcome various hardships to fearlessly benefit others.

Many people think that bodhisattvas are just statues in temples. This isn't the case. For the sake of others, they gave up their own interests and incarnated in this world. As long as they can help others, they willingly bear any mistreatment, such as being disdained, satirized, or misunderstood. This is the bodhisattva in real life.

In Qinghai province, there's a monastic who has been called a bodhisattva. Why? Because though he leads an extremely simple life, as long as people need his help, he does his utmost to help them. Even when he's treated unjustly, he doesn't care.

Everyone needs this spirit. Modern education always focuses on how to be successful and how to make huge profits, but rarely mentions how to benefit others. I guess it's not difficult to imagine how our society is going to turn out.

Obviously, the altruistic mind is a vast subject, so it's hard to completely understand it in such a short time. Nevertheless, I still hope you realize that the altruistic mind is like a wish-fulfilling jewel: the rays that it emanates can dispel the darkness of ignorance in human hearts and illuminate the correct path for our life. Never ignore its importance.

Q&A

Would you please address how to practice bodhichitta?
There are many methods. Specifically, there are methods for practicing aspiration bodhichitta and methods for action bodhichitta, as well as methods for developing the equality of self and other, such as through the exchange of self and other. For detailed steps, you can refer to *A Guide to the Preliminary Practices of the Great Perfection* (or *Words of My Perfect Teacher*) and *Finding Comfort and Ease in the Nature of Mind*.

To make it simple, though, at any time and any place, you can practice in this way: give away all your happiness to all sentient beings and take upon yourself all the suffering of sentient beings. The point of this practice is to greatly decrease self-attachment.

Some people may think that this is scary and may worry, "If others have some disease, will I get it?" In fact, this worry is totally unnecessary. Through the mighty power of bodhichitta, you'll obtain inconceivable benefit instead.

How can I find correct direction in life?
We don't live just a single lifetime; we'll experience many lifetimes. Thus, I recommend you learn some Buddhist theories. There's no harm in doing so.

I've skimmed the Buddhist canonical literature and a great number of ancient and modern books from China and other countries. Comparing these, I've noticed that Buddhism offers incomparable guidance for life. Thus, I suggest you find your direction through Buddhism.

Would you please describe the difference between Chinese and Tibetan Buddhism based on what you've seen and heard in Tibet and China?

In the past, Chinese people had very little exposure to Tibetan Buddhism. In 1987, when my teacher Kyabjé Jigme Phuntsok Rinpoché visited the holy Mount Wutai, many Chinese people started to connect with Tibetan Buddhism.

Chinese Buddhism has always emphasized a vegetarian diet, meditation, and chanting the names of buddhas. In this aspect, it has exceeded Tibetan Buddhism. On the other hand, Tibetan Buddhism has systematic and thorough study and practice curricula. So, students can gradually study Buddhadharma from a basic to an advanced level. Plus, it utilizes debate in order to dispel all sorts of doubts and confusion. In this way, students gain a solid foundation for practice. Moreover, in order to be qualified to propagate the Dharma, teachers in Tibetan Buddhism must go through long-term trainings in teaching, debating, and composing, as well as strict authentication in their disciplines. Thus, they have reached a relatively high standard of Buddhist studies.

Generally speaking, both Chinese and Tibetan Buddhism are forms of Mahayana Buddhism, so they don't differ too much. However, I hope that Chinese Buddhism will start to propagate Buddhist theories not only in monasteries, but also among common people and in universities. Many Chinese Buddhists are very devoted. When they visit monasteries, they make prostrations to the buddha statues, offer incense, and take refuge, but they don't understand why they do this. This is a little bit naive.

Some Buddhists, when asked whether they follow Mahayana or Theravada Buddhism, or the great or basic vehicles, proudly claim that they're studying Mahayana Buddhism. However, when they're asked what distinguishes these, they have no idea. The answer is actually very simple: the only criterion to distinguish them is altruistic bodhichitta. Without bodhichitta, even if you build many monasteries and perform virtuous deeds, it's not Mahayana Buddhism.

It's a pity that many Buddhists put on a façade of studying Dharma while only a small number are really learning it deeply.

In Tibet, is there any religion that has conflicts with Buddhism? Within Buddhism, are there conflicts among different schools and sects?
In Tibet, there aren't many religions besides Buddhism. In recent years, a few more have appeared, but so far, none of them have become popular in Tibet.

Buddhism began to flourish in Tibet in the sixth century. Although it has gone through difficulties and challenges, such as suppression by the King Langdarma, the pure transmission has been perfectly preserved. It has even attracted many foreign scholars to study it.

Within Tibetan Buddhism, there are eight schools, including Geluk, Sakya, Nyingma, Kagyu, Jonang, and so forth. In the past, there were conflicts among the different schools, but now, all the schools are in great harmony and agree that the path of practice starts with generating bodhichitta, requires accumulating merit in the middle, and ends with attaining Buddhahood. Therefore, there's no conflict in terms of the general teachings of the different schools.

We're Tibetan students at Shandong University. Khenpo, thank you very much for coming here to lecture. We also thank our school for providing this great opportunity for us. We're so excited!

It's through the internet that we got to know you. We watched the videos of you releasing captive animals back into the wild and great sympathy arose in us. Now we also regularly study your recorded teachings. Our question is this: Studying in mainland China, what should we keep in mind?

Also, we're enthusiastic to study Dharma online, and we're very earnest and active. Would you please put more teachings in Tibetan language on your website?

It's not easy for you to study here so far from your own home. Shandong is the cradle of Confucianism, which has also influenced mainstream Chinese culture for several thousand years, just like Buddhism in Tibet. Since you're studying here, please cherish this opportunity and never waste time.

Not long ago, I mentioned at a university in Qinghai province that these days some Tibetan students don't value their own traditional culture. Rather, it's the Chinese professors and students who are particularly interested in studying Tibetan Buddhism. This is really shameful. I hope that while you're studying the many excellent aspects of Chinese culture here in this university, you don't forsake Tibetan Buddhism.

Another thing that's worth mentioning is that some Tibetan students, including some college students financially supported by me, completely forget the Tibetan language after they study in Chinese areas. As far as I know, many Chinese students study abroad, but when they come back to visit their parents, they still speak Chinese, not English. Why do

Tibetan students not act in this way? I hope you keep this in mind.

In regard to Tibetan study materials, I've posted some on my Tibetan Weibo (microblog) and Tibetan Blog. Also, I have a website called the Wisdom and Compassion Buddhist Website. It has a Tibetan version. With it, I hope to propagate Tibetan Buddhism and culture, and meanwhile, integrate Buddhism and modern issues. I believe young people will find it useful.

I've read some Buddhist books, but when I encounter problems, the first thought that comes to me is still "me." I realize I'm still very self-centered, so I feel bad about it. How can I really apply bodhichitta in my daily life?
It's a very difficult process. However, we should still try to practice step by step.

I myself have studied Buddhism for a long time. However, when something happens, my first thought is often still "me," so I'm very ashamed. To counter this, it's good to read the biographies of great masters, such as Venerable Atisha, and to emulate their conduct little by little, so that our self-attachment will gradually weaken. At the beginning, we may think of "me" every day, but after we understand the importance of altruism and the harm of self-attachment, we'll stop thinking of "me" so often.

Obviously, we can't achieve this in a couple of days or years. Only through practicing step by step with perseverance can we reach a point where we'll naturally think of all sentient beings instead of "me" no matter the place or time.

This is the experience of many great masters since ancient times, including the great masters from our Buddhist insti-

tute. At the beginning, they also put great effort into training themselves to put the benefit of sentient beings first and
foremost whenever they spoke or took action. Then gradually they mastered bodhichitta.

When I studied your Great Commentary on the Preliminary
Practices of the Great Perfection, *I was very motivated and got
up at 5:30 AM every day to do the related meditations, but after
a couple of months, indolence and boredom arose, so I scolded
myself. A Dharma brother said, "This is normal; the greater your
motivation, the greater the unfavorable conditions." Where did
this statement come from?*

First of all, I admire your effort, but I don't agree that the
greater the motivation, the greater the unfavorable conditions.

It's been said that "as virtue raises one foot, vice raises
ten," and worldly people also say, "A tall tree attracts wind,"
which means that when one is successful in business or
practice, more unfavorable conditions appear. But this isn't
always the case. It also sometimes happens that when some
practitioners are doing great, all unfavorable conditions vanish completely.

Nonetheless, it's normal that you practice diligently when
you first start studying Buddhadharma and become a little
bit lazy as time goes on. When you understand the importance of practice and experience the actual benefits of it,
you'll never give up. I believe that the more diligently one
practices, the less unfavorable conditions one will have and
the sooner accomplishments will come.

I often see people sell fish and turtles on the roadside, and my first thought is to save these creatures, but as the saying goes, "No business, no killing." Releasing wildlife is also a "business," so I hesitate to buy them, and even think more extremely that maybe these people deliberately catch them for us to buy them for releasing. What should I do?

Business doesn't necessarily cause killing. Releasing wildlife is an example. Analyze every issue based on its specific conditions.

Of course, there are people who do catch fish and birds in order to sell them to us to release. However, even if this is the case, life is still most precious. No matter what, we should still put saving lives first.

Nonetheless, it's good to pay attention to these issues while releasing wildlife. We don't have to release them at regular times. If we're predictable, then the business-minded will figure this out and catch lots of creatures and ask for higher prices on, say, the first and the fifteenth of each lunar month or on Buddhist holidays. Deliberately avoid those days, and release wildlife on any other day. If we release wildlife randomly in this way, those people won't be able to catch creatures especially for us. Thus, the problem that concerns you is resolved.

Lecture at Shandong University
November 16, 2011

7. THE BUDDHIST LOW-DESIRE, LOW-CARBON LIFESTYLE

In recent decades, under the influence of the slogan "human wisdom can prevail over nature" and in order to satisfy their increasing desire, people began exploiting natural resources unscrupulously. This has caused grave damage to our environment.

TODAY I HAVE feelings of sadness and joy.

What makes me sad is that fifteen years ago, I accompanied my teacher to visit Guangxi and served as his translator and attendant. We stayed beside the Yong River for a couple of days, and my teacher taught Buddhadharma to fortunate people and released creatures at Qingxiu Mountain. Today, revisiting this place, past scenes fill my mind, but my teacher isn't here anymore, so I have an indescribable feeling.

What brings me joy is that twenty years ago, I talked with several professors at Guangxi University who were studying Buddhadharma and seeking to understand the mysteries of the mind. Today, I'm very gratified to learn that they're still exploring this field. Studying Buddhadharma requires long-term perseverance. A short period of enthusiasm won't bring about accomplishment.

Why do monastics go out into the secular world?

Some people may think, "Monastics should stay in monasteries. Why associate with worldly people?"

This question only reflects their lack of Buddhist knowledge. Other than my apparel and values, I'm not so different from you.

Buddhism can be divided into the Great Vehicle (Mahayana) and the Basic Vehicle (Theravada). On the Basic Vehicle, monastics only seek self-liberation, so they meditate deep in the mountains and restrain their conduct to the point of not even touching money. In contrast, the Great Vehicle promotes not only self-liberation but also freeing sentient beings from all kinds of suffering. As long as an action benefits sentient beings, it's permitted and even required.

For myself, as a Mahayana practitioner, I can't just seek self-liberation. As one of seven billion citizens on earth, I have an urgent responsibility to confront issues we're facing. For instance, I've been concerned about environmental protection for years, attending forums and exchanging ideas with experts from various countries, and I often reflect on current environmental changes and their consequences.

The earth is sick.

What's wrong with the earth?

First of all, there's severe water pollution. Seventy percent of the rivers in China are polluted. Once I observed an experiment with a water purifier in Shanghai in which 30 percent of the tap water was left as precipitate. If people drink this kind of water, all that precipitate must be detoxified by our livers and kidneys. What a burden for our body!

From outer space, the earth is a blue planet with three-fourths of its surface area covered by water. Only 2.53 percent of this water is drinkable freshwater, and this number is gradually decreasing. The Qinghai-Tibet Plateau has been called "the water tower of Asia" because it's the source of the Yangtze River, Yellow River, and Ganges River. However, due to global warming, the glaciers on the plateau are dramatically melting away. Water will surely be a great worry for us in the future.

Second, the forest area is also quickly shrinking. It only takes a couple minutes to cut down a tree, but it takes decades for it to grow. Massive deforestation directly leads to an abnormal climate. The drought in Yunnan has affected several million people and it's said that the world's biggest paper mill in this province is one of the causes.

Further, drought often results in famine. To the south of the Sahara Desert in the Sahel, ten to fourteen million people suffer food shortages and over one million children less than five years old suffer severe malnutrition.

Moreover, issues like the thinning ozone layer, soil destruction, species extinction, and overexploitation of natural resources make the idea of pristine mountains and rivers and perfectly clear skies all seem like fairy tales.

Maybe it's just my own groundless fear, but I often think that if we keep disrespecting nature like this, our generation will experience even greater disasters.

Can twenty earths be enough?

Environmental problems result from multiple causes. However, the root cause stems mainly from human desire's endless reach, especially regarding food, housing, and transportation. Without a sense of thrift, waste will overwhelm us.

Not long ago, I went to a city on Chinese New Year's Eve. Normally we think of this as a joyous time of reuniting with loved ones, but it wasn't joyous at all. The sound of firecrackers was earsplitting and really annoying. From just this one night of firecracker explosions there was serious air pollution. Moreover, the large amount of firecracker debris was a huge burden for the poor sanitation workers.

Some people believe it's an extremely honorable thing to place a lot of food on the dinner table, so they order over a thousand or even ten thousand dollars' worth of food, but then only eat a small part of it. In regard to clothing, they're too picky and believe that it's a symbol of their status. I know one rich man who has too many luxurious clothes to wear them all.

Buddhism teaches that it's important to cherish and conserve things. For instance, a Buddhist sutra says that monastics shouldn't throw away old clothes. Rather, when clothes are worn out, they should use them to make cushions; when the cushions are tattered, they should use the fabric for duster cloths; when the duster cloths are unusable, they should mix them with mortar to plaster walls. Among some old practitioners, this tradition has still been preserved. In Larung Gar, I know an old teacher who has worn one of his clothing items since 1987. There's another khenpo who has a teapot that he has used for over thirty years.

However, modern people seem to believe that squandering is honorable and thrift is shameful. If someone is thrifty, they look down on him and call him stingy. Sadly, sometimes these economical people start to believe that it's indeed disgraceful to be thrifty.

At every meal, reflect on the series of difficulties that were required for that food to be in front of you. With every thread, ponder the toil it took to bring it to you. If everybody sought a life of luxury, how many natural resources would we need? Some experts have calculated that if everyone in the world used the same amount of resources as the average American, we would need at least twenty earths to support us.

You're not the earth's master.

In *Earth in the Balance*, Al Gore, the former US vice president, mentioned that the conflict between world civilizations and the earth's ecosystem stems from three things: the population explosion, the scientific and technological revolution, and the devaluation of nature.

He makes a great point with this last one. Something has gone wrong with how we view nature.

In the past, Chinese people advocated that we humans live as one with nature. They revered nature to a great extent. Green mountains and rivers were everywhere—even in poetry and art. Later, influenced by the slogan "human wisdom can prevail over nature" and in order to satisfy their increasing desire, people began exploiting natural resources unscrupulously. This has caused grave damage to our environment.

Take fishing for example. In the past, people fished with barbs and each time only caught what they needed for the day. Nowadays, fishermen use a massive dragnet to catch the whole lot of fish in an entire sea area.

Currently over seventy species of insects or animals become extinct every day. Every hour, three species leave us forever and become another victim of ecological destruction. Suppose one day all those beings who swim in oceans, fly in the sky, and run on the ground become extinct. How long will we human beings be able to survive?

Some people believe that we're the masters of the earth, so we have the right to dictate everything. This view is really mindless. It has been estimated that the earth is as old as 4.6 billion years, while human beings only appeared several million years ago. Obviously, we aren't the earth's masters, and we're not qualified to do whatever we want to it.

Low-carbon living can only result from less desire.

In order to protect the earth, many people advocate for adopting a low-carbon lifestyle, but how can we do this? It's simple: less desire means less carbon output.

In Tibet, people eat simple food, live in plain rooms, and wear a single piece of clothing for many years. They don't have much desire, so they always wear smiles on their faces, and melodious songs always resound through the mountains there. This low-desire lifestyle is indeed low-carbon.

In order to reach this state, mere wishes aren't enough, so it's better to understand some Buddhadharma and let go of desire skillfully.

What I'm saying may alarm some people, and they may think, "This is his multilevel marketing scheme. He just wants to get us to study Buddhadharma!" Such wariness is unnecessary. You can analyze by yourself whether Buddhadharma is reasonable or not. If it does make sense and can make people happy, even if you don't want to follow it, at least it doesn't hurt for you to learn about it.

Over twenty-five hundred years ago, through his wisdom, the Buddha revealed the nature of all phenomena. For example, he taught the *Kalachakra* (*Wheel of Time*) in southern India. According to the calculation methods in this teaching, the precise times for solar and lunar eclipses can be predicted without any instruments. Moreover, some theories found in quantum mechanics were already explained by the Buddha in his teachings on understanding dependent origination as emptiness.

What does this mean? Buddhism isn't as simple as some people assume.

In fact, all sorts of current problems, whether external or internal, can be answered by Buddhism. Take environmental protection for example. The inner protection advocated by Buddhism is more essential than environmental protection in this time. Why? The root cause of our environmental problems isn't carbon but desire. When you see others wear Chanel, you want to wear it too; when others buy an iPhone, you want to purchase one too; when others own a BMW, you want to drive one too. Have you ever thought about how many natural resources all of these require?

Mahatma Gandhi once said, "Earth provides enough to satisfy every man's need, but not every man's greed."

Desire is indeed scary. Our desire-driven actions may not immediately result in destruction, but just like frogs cooked in warm water, we'll not be able to escape once we realize what's going on.

Obviously, to restrain desire doesn't mean to force everyone to shave their heads and live in monasteries. Actually, we human beings can live a very comfortable life with moderate material conditions. It's enough to have some clothes to cover and keep our bodies warm. It's unnecessary to have luxurious food, clothes, and houses. Instead, cultivate satisfaction. In our Buddhist institute, some practitioners have lived happily in a tiny lodge for over twenty years.

Thus, it's good and necessary for everyone to reflect, "Do I really need to indulge my desire?"

Happiness is a feeling.

In order to find happiness, people buy more and more, but since this approach is incorrect, no matter how much they own, they never find contentment.

In the US, in a city by the sea, there lives a very successful Chinese woman. Once, one of her high school classmates called her and wanted to visit her while on business in the States. She was so happy that she drove her luxurious car to the airport to pick up her classmate in person.

Upon arriving at her house, her classmate saw a mansion, a swimming pool, a tennis court, a well-maintained garden, and a luxurious sports car. After entering the mansion, there were more than a dozen rooms, all with rare calligraphies and paintings on the wall.

However, the empty house confused her classmate. "Where's your family?"

She answered, "A couple of years ago, my husband had an affair and left me. My children have grown up and have their own dreams, so they moved out. Now, I have nothing but money . . ."

Happiness doesn't mean vast wealth and abundant material goods. Rather, happiness is a mindset of contentment—a feeling that doesn't require many things.

All happiness originates from our heart. To protect the environment, start with your heart. The current destruction of the environment is a result of human greed. Without achieving less desire, no matter how much we advocate for low-carbon living, it will only fail to improve things. Only when we pinpoint the root of the problem can the damage to the environment be lessened, and can people begin to experience genuine happiness.

Q&A

In recent years, an abnormal global climate has caused various secondary disasters. Some researchers suggest that this is the result of the industrialization of the past several hundred years.

My question is this: Can we really stop the deterioration of the environment by restraining human desire?

It's impossible to put a complete stop to environmental deterioration right away, but as long as we make an effort, there must be some effect.

It was reported by the UN that one of the major causes of global warming is satisfying the human demand for meat. In order to meet this demand, livestock farming has rapidly developed and has become the chief offender of climate change. If everyone were vegetarian, it would lessen global warming by 80 percent. In this regard, vegetarianism isn't just a Buddhist act.

I think college students have a strong awareness of environmental protection, but entrepreneurs don't, so most of the environmental pollution is caused by the latter. How can we enhance their awareness of environmental protection?

"Environmental protection" is a relatively new term. I remember when I was young there was no such term. Air and water were pure and clean, and I had never even seen a trash bin. In the past several decades, with the development of the economy, we have polluted our environment in numerous ways, so people have started paying attention to environmental protection.

In order to enhance awareness of environmental protection among entrepreneurs, we need help from academia. In our current society, we have three important groups of people: officials, entrepreneurs, and scholars. Most problems are first recognized by scholars. Although entrepreneurs and officials have money and power, they're busy with making money and decisions, so they don't have time to think about long-term consequences. Therefore, scholars need to reveal these critical problems to entrepreneurs and officials.

For instance, when universities hold environmental protection forums, they can invite entrepreneurs and officials so that they learn about the importance of environmental protection. If they have a better sense of this, it will be more likely for them to take the appropriate measures.

Because of today's lecture, I feel more strongly about environmental protection. However, I know my mind is fickle, so I may go back to being environmentally unfriendly after a couple of days. What should I do?
If you have truly realized the importance of environmental protection, you won't forget it for the rest of your life. I myself have had such experiences: sometimes when I listened to a lecture from my teacher, my mind would undergo such a tremendous change that from then on, I always remembered it firmly.

If you don't feel very strongly, then you need to reflect repeatedly. Otherwise, what touches you right now may vanish after a couple of days without any trace.

What I have mentioned today can only work as a reminder for you. The key is to put in the effort yourself.

I will graduate in two years. The competition is fierce and everyone is pursuing money, so if I keep a kind heart, I may not be able to make enough money to support my family. What should I do if this happens?
A good conscience doesn't necessarily prevent you from making money. Some entrepreneurs have a very strong altruistic mind and sense of responsibility for society, but

the money they make isn't less than others. To survive in this society doesn't require inappropriate approaches.

In the process of making a living, if you make money at the expense of others, it will not last long. If you work with a kind heart and a clear conscience, your merit will certainly and steadily increase. In any case, even if you can't make money right away, don't give up a kind heart. In the long run, a kind heart will be more beneficial for you.

Lecture at Guangxi University
February 27, 2012

8. SELFLESS HEARTS EXPAND

The reason to study Dharma isn't to seek blessings for the self. Rather, it's for giving up the self. The reason to beseech the Buddha isn't to gain wealth but to give up attachment to wealth. The reason to beseech the Buddha isn't to obtain a long life but to give up clinging to this body. The reason to beseech the Buddha isn't to eradicate demons but to give up hatred and to treat them with great compassion.

NOBODY WANTS SUFFERING; everybody wishes for happiness. However, our life seldom follows our wishes. So, when we inevitably encounter frustrations and misfortunes, rather than blaming others and cursing fate, try to understand suffering, look for its root, and then search for a solution. This is what the Buddha did 2,500 years ago.

Many people associate Buddhism with the phrase "life is full of suffering." But how many really analyze this statement and wonder, "What's the root of all the suffering in our life?" When you're suffering, either physically or mentally, whether about relationships or your career, where does this suffering really come from?

The answer is that it comes from attachment to this "self."

I didn't quite understand this point when I was in school, but still I had a vague idea that suffering must involve the mind. Only after I became a monk did I realize that suffering isn't only related to mind; it's directly associated with self-attachment.

The Indian scholar Shantideva states, "Self-attachment only increases suffering." The *Seven Points of Mind Training*, by Geshe Chekawa Yeshe Dorje, also pushes us to attribute all our suffering to self-attachment, rather than to blame other people, circumstances, or things.

People with strong self-attachment are rather small-hearted. They can't tolerate a slight wrong and easily lose their temper. As the saying goes, "Noblemen have a great mental capacity, while disgraceful people have great anger." If we have strong self-attachment and are unable to put objectionable occurrences out of our minds, then even if we owned the entire world, we still wouldn't stop complaining. If we're not very attached to the self, however, and generally never fuss about anything, then even if we were so poor that we owned only one bed, our hearts would still be full of gratitude.

Just as the Japanese Zen Master Muso Soseki stated, "If grit is in your eyes, even the three realms appear small; if nothing settles in your heart, even one bed is wide enough." Most of our problems, whether as trivial as family arguments or as significant as world wars, can all trace their root cause to self-attachment.

Now that the problem is clear, how do we uproot this self-attachment? The first thing to examine is this "self" that we all cling to. Is it real or not?

Plato's *Republic*, Book VII, gives a very good analogy that answers this question. It's known as the Allegory of the Cave:

Many generations of people had lived in a cave. From birth, they lived like prisoners, chained to the wall of the cave, with their necks and legs fixed. They couldn't turn their heads to look around or behind. Thus, they could only look at the cave wall in front of them.

Behind them was a fire, and another group of people who all carried objects. The prisoners, however, could only see the shadow of these objects cast upon the opposite wall. They had no idea there was a fire or other people.

Since they looked at these shadows every day, they gradually believed that these shadowy objects were real objects. As they didn't know of the world beyond their cave and their chains, they never thought to escape.

One day, a prisoner was freed from the chains and walked out of the cave. He saw light for the first time in his life. Once his eyes adjusted, he was able to see everything, even the sun. He realized that what they had been seeing on the cave wall was only a shadow and not at all real.

He felt fortunate that he had escaped and was sympathetic toward those still in the cave. He returned to the cave, but nobody believed him; they all agreed that he had been made crazy and decided that if anyone were to free them from their chains and try to drag them away, they would beat that person to death.

What does this story imply? The things that people consider to be unquestionably real may be the most unreal.

Why did people not trust the prisoner who walked out of the cave and clearly saw reality? As it's said in the *Dream of the Red Chamber*, "When unreal is considered real, real becomes unreal; when absence is viewed as presence, presence turns into absence."

This is also true for the "self" that we sentient beings cling to; it appears to exist, yet it's really only like shadows cast upon a cave wall.

Some people may doubt this, saying, "If it was only me who clung to an intrinsic 'self,' I could admit that I'm wrong. However, every single being in this world clings to an intrinsic 'self'—how can we all be wrong?"

The ancient Indian scholar Chandrakirti tells a story in his *Commentary on the Four Hundred Stanzas on the Middle Way* that addresses this:

Once upon a time, a Brahmin told a king that a couple days later there would be a cursed rain. People who drank that rain would become crazy. After a few days, it indeed rained, and everyone in this kingdom drank the rain and became crazy except the king. However, since he was the only one who was different from all the other people, he was called a madman. Having no other choice, the king finally had to drink the rain and become the same as all the other people.

We might think this is ridiculous, but unfortunately, this is exactly what we're experiencing right now. Since the "self" is unreal and attachment toward it only brings suffering, the only way to be happy is to give up this "self."

Chinese characters were developed by ancient people in an interesting way. In the character 我 ("self" or "I") is hidden a dangerous weapon: 戈 ("dagger" or "spear"). As long as there's "self" or "I," this weapon can harm others as well as oneself.

So how do we deal with this "self" and eliminate self-attachment?

In the wisdom chapter in the *Guide to the Bodhisattva's Way of Life*, Shantideva scrutinizes the theory of selflessness using logical reasoning. For instance, if we examine each part of our body one after another—hair, teeth, arms, legs, and so forth—we'll easily understand that we can't find a "self" in any part of the body. Since the self can't be found, what basis is there for attachment? In this way, self-attachment is refuted.

Alternatively, you can also use the method of contemplating a specific question. In the Zen school, the question is "Who am I?" and in secret Tantrayana, the question is "Where am I?" Relying on these questions, people with the highest faculties will suddenly realize that "I," and everything that "I" is attached to, doesn't exist at all.

Of course, to reach such realization requires a long-term commitment to Dharma study and practice.

But among all the methods of giving up attachment to this self, the best one is simply to benefit others.

It's said in the *Spring and Autumn of Lu*, "The sky is selfless, so it covers; the earth is selfless, so it carries; the sun and the moon are selfless, so they illuminate; the four seasons are selfless, so they proceed well." Human beings should emulate the sky and the earth, eliminating the selfish thinking of self-clinging.

When the altruistic mind is enhanced, selfishness weakens; when selfishness is weakened, altruism becomes stronger. Thus, in the progression of enhancing altruism and weakening selfishness, our suffering will likewise decrease.

It might be difficult at the beginning, but as long as you remind yourself to put aside yourself and think more of others, you'll gradually realize that this produces the happiest and the most relaxed mental state.

The meaning of our life isn't to accumulate money, but to benefit others and eventually all sentient beings. How do we benefit others? Bring happiness to those who lack happiness; eliminate suffering from those who are suffering.

Obviously, as ordinary beings, it's unrealistic to be completely altruistic because we all still have attachment toward the "self." Even though this is unavoidable, we can at least stop handing over the reins to our self-attachment. If we think only of ourselves day and night without considering others for even a moment, our space will never be vast. And for others, our existence may not have any value.

What kind of people offer value to the world? Altruistic people. Altruism touches everybody, and what touches people most is the altruism in Mahayana Buddhism, for it involves unconditionally benefiting every sentient being.

For common people, benefiting others is more like a deal: when I help you, I expect you to help me later. This isn't the case for

Mahayana Buddhism. In Mahayana Buddhism, benefiting others is unconditional. As long as sentient beings have suffering, we make an all-out effort to help and are willing to do it at any cost. For most of us, this is out of reach, but still most admirable.

Uprooting self-attachment doesn't just reduce suffering but also helps us realize the truth of all phenomena—emptiness.

Some people don't understand what's meant by emptiness and think, "Buddhism talks about emptiness, but if everything is empty, should we even bother with our life and career?" The answer is yes. Emptiness doesn't mean nothingness. Rather, it means that everything around us, including ourselves, is empty of inherent nature but still appears. Thus, we still have to be responsible for what we're engaged in. If, however, we understand that everything is empty by nature, our selfish thinking decreases and our world expands.

Q&A

Nowadays there's a lot of eroticism online, and in classic Western art, nakedness is viewed as beautiful. Modern people also like to expose themselves, baring any part of their bodies they can. I'm so confused. What's your opinion on this?

I guess people in the East who view nakedness as beautiful could be under the influence of Western culture, but this is debatable. There are many instances of eroticism in the East. To name a few: the *Kama Sutra*, temple goddesses throughout South and Southeast Asia, or even Japanese paintings of geishas. Online pornography and the trend toward miniskirts and bare midriffs in its modern rendition might be more of a Western cultural phenomenon, but viewing the naked human body, especially the female human body, as beautiful, seems neither Eastern nor Western.

If we analyze the body, whether female or male, through meditation on the unclean, none of it's worth lusting over. Unfortunately, ordinary people have a habitual tendency toward lust, so businesspeople take advantage of this weakness, attracting people's eyes with naked bodies in order to increase profits.

As time goes on, however, people will go back to their traditional ways. Why? When something gets too popular, its disadvantages become obvious, and people will definitely start to reexamine all this.

Some Buddhists are eager to introduce Buddhadharma to others. They often talk so much about the law of karmic cause and effect and forcefully give advice that it has the opposite result. Actually, young people like a more literary and relaxed style— why do they have to rigidly push Buddhism onto people?
I've noticed this too, but not everyone acts in this way.

Buddhism has a very rich body of knowledge. In Tibetan Buddhism, there are ten *vidyas*, or classes of knowledge. Among them, there are five major vidyas, or sciences: the science of language, the science of logic, the science of fine arts and crafts, the science of medicine, and the science of spirituality. There are also five minor vidyas or sciences: the science of rhetoric, the science of lexicon, the science of prosody, the science of drama, and the science of calendar calculation. Many of these studies are closely associated with modern arts and sciences. If one knows how to apply this knowledge, there are a variety of ways to guide people.

Truly great masters use different skillful means to suit the different interests of people. Whether in the East or the West, their approaches are very well acknowledged. People who wish to propagate Buddhadharma need some qualifications. In the secular world, people can be successful when they have certain academic degrees and experience; morality is often not a criterion. In Buddhism, however, besides mastery of Buddhadharma, one must have pure precepts, and an actual realization of meditation; a silver tongue isn't enough.

I'm from Gansu University of Chinese Medicine, studying traditional medicine and culture. I've been to some Tibetan hospitals and learned that Tibetan medicine is a crucial part of Tibetan Buddhism. Would you please give a brief introduction to it?
Among the five sciences in Tibetan Buddhism, the science of medicine is what we call "Tibetan medicine."

Tibetan medicine is held in great esteem internationally. It has distinctive qualities from prescription to treatment. I was so interested in it when I was in school that I studied how to feel the pulse, pharmaceutics, and collecting herbs on mountains. Tibet has abundant medicinal resources. As one saying goes, "None of the plants on the mountains aren't medicines in the eyes of a brilliant doctor." At that time, my dream was to be a doctor, but after I took ordination in our Buddhist institute, I mostly stopped studying it.

Ancient Tibetan medicine has well-developed medical care techniques. In Xining, Qinghai, there's a Tibetan medicinal culture museum, in which a great number of sophisticated medical care instruments are displayed, some of which have a history of over a thousand years.

Nowadays, Tibetan medicine has been passed on through Tibetan hospitals. Our Buddhist institute has also trained many doctors and even established cooperation with some nursing schools and medical schools.

Some diseases that Western or Chinese medicine can't cure may be cured by seeing Tibetan doctors and taking Tibetan medicine. I myself like to take Tibetan medicine when I get sick; the side effects are almost nonexistent and the result is quite good.

If you're interested in studying Tibetan medicine, the *Four Medical Treatises* is an essential scripture. If you can master the theories in it, you can nurse your own health and feel confident to cure the sickness of others.

In Confucianism, Mencius held the theory that people are by nature good, while Xunzi believed that people are by nature bad. What's the Buddhist point of view on human nature?
The philosophies of Confucianism and Buddhism are in some ways interlinked. For example, both philosophies suggest that there's an invisible human nature.

Some scholars explain this with a metaphor: an object in a dark room without light can't be discovered, but once the room is illuminated, the object is seen. Human nature is the same.

Mencius and Xunzi's views on human nature are that it's either good or bad. In Buddhism, however, human nature transcends good and bad at the ultimate level because everything is equal and free from dualism.

At a beginner's level, however, Buddhism also posits that human nature is good. Why? Because everyone has buddha nature and can become a buddha. This was clearly expounded in the *Tathagatagarbha Sutra* and *Uttaratantra*.

If human nature were bad, then no matter how much effort we made to become good, we would eventually degenerate. The thousands of enlightened beings, like Buddha Shakyamuni and Master Huineng (the Six Patriarch) have proved that this is false with their personal realization. When mind returns to its primordial state, the bright side will definitely appear.

Confucianism states, "If three walk together, at least one can be my teacher." Buddhism also believes that everyone can be one's teacher. How can we reach such a state?
When one reaches a certain level of realization, everyone's conduct and speech become beneficial instructions. Even when cursed, such people don't feel hurt. Rather, they take it as the best teaching and correct their mistakes. If we can likewise do this, everyone can be our teacher.

Without this realization, let alone criticism, even praise may sound sarcastic. In this way, it's hard to view anyone as a teacher. These people don't even think their teachers are really teachers. Just like childish students, they mock teachers after class. So, in their eyes, even teachers aren't teachers at all.

"If three walk together, at least one can be my teacher" isn't a basic level of realization. This is actually similar to what's called pure vision in Buddhism. Venerable Atisha once said, "Among three people, at least one must be a bodhisattva." This means that the proportion of bodhisattvas is fairly high, but it's a pity that we can't perceive them. Who is and who isn't? We don't know.

With a pure mind, everyone is a bodhisattva in your eyes. Without it, everyone is inferior to you. Living in this way, there's only suffering and no happiness.

I studied Buddhadharma under some teachers and read their

books, but later I found them slandering tantric teachings. How should I treat them?
They slandered tantric teachings only because they don't understand them.

Tantric teachings aren't simple. There are vast numbers of tantras and commentaries in Tibetan Buddhism. Even after a dozen years of study you still may not fully understand them, but once you do, you'll be astonished and think, "Ah, I was so stupid before!"

Setting aside ordinary teachers, even some great masters like Master Hong Yi didn't understand tantric teachings in the beginning. After they read the secret tantras and their instructions by great Tibetan masters, however, they all confessed their misunderstandings.

I can understand where these teachers are coming from. They readily slander tantra under the influence of their environment and friends, as well as due to their lack of study of tantra. I would hope they could go to the Buddhist institutes in Tibet to meet and debate with Buddhists there. If they win, we give up. However, if they don't even understand basic Buddhist logical reasoning but only insist on their own view, then it can't be justified.

Buddhism emphasizes the importance on having faith in the teacher and the Three Jewels, but it's very difficult for beginners to gain stable and irreversible faith. Do you have any suggestions?
There are two approaches to gaining faith in the teacher and the Three Jewels:

First is relying on karmic connections from past lives. If one studied or practiced Dharma in former lives, then it will not be too difficult to gain faith in this life.

Second is to read extensively the biographies of buddhas, bodhisattvas, and past great masters, and to study earnestly the Buddhadharma, especially the teaching on emptiness.

The *Four Hundred Stanzas on the Middle Way* states that if you doubt the teachings of the Buddha, studying his teachings on emptiness will help you to gain genuine faith. Why? The teachings on emptiness are the most profound. Even the smartest person in the world couldn't reveal it. Only the Buddha is able to perceive it and teach it.

Once you're convinced through logic and reasoning, irreversible faith will naturally arise.

I'm a sophomore and very busy with my studies. How can I find time to recite more prayers?

Mr. Lu Xun said, "Time is like the water in a sponge; if you squeeze it, more comes out." As long as it doesn't affect your studies, use your spare time in the morning and at night to study Buddhadharma.

Dharma study isn't just reciting prayers. What's more important is to learn the meaning of Buddhadharma. Currently, the study of Buddhist scriptures is insufficient in China. The collection of canonical works sits on the shelf and very few people are willing to dive into it. This is quite a shame.

To study the Dharma is to study the wisdom of Buddha Shakyamuni. To read his words is to be benefited infinitely.

There have been many religions from ancient times until now. How can different religions get along with one another?

Different religions, as well as believers and nonbelievers,

should respect, understand, and learn from one another. Any religion that has survived in this world until now must have vital force and charm. If one religion is incompatible with other religions, it won't exist for very long.

How should we treat dreams?
Life is a dream. The way you treat your life should be the way you treat dreams.

I'm an instructor from Gansu University. I'm planning to establish a meditation center in our school to help students correctly understand Buddhism and cultivate loving-kindness and compassion. What curricula and activities would you recommend?
It's better to integrate Zen culture in these kinds of centers. There are Zen Buddhist societies in Peking University and Fudan University; there's a Center for Spirit and Cognition Studies in Central China Normal University. If you decide to initiate one, start with Zen.

The practice of bodhichitta in Tibetan Buddhism is also very practical. Bodhichitta calls for altruism, which can calm our minds. Why? Restlessness, worries, and anxiety all are rooted in self-attachment. When altruism arises, self-attachment spontaneously weakens, and suffering will decrease.

In regard to activities, you can invite some professors who are proficient in both Chinese and Tibetan Buddhism to give lectures. It can greatly benefit society if students can cultivate loving-kindness and compassion.

Recently, professors from various universities met to discuss how to enhance the comprehensive qualities— especially traditional morality—of students. What they're doing is indeed helpful for students! With such education, even if the students can't find a job in the end, they can at least determine the goal of their life. It's difficult to solve all of life's problems with high test scores.

I'm very interested in Buddhism, so I read a great number of Buddhist books, but I haven't yet obtained much in the way of understanding. How can I develop a comprehensive understanding of Buddhism? Could you please recommend some Buddhist books?

No matter what we study, gaining a superficial understanding from cursory observation will not do. Without diving deeply into a subject, we can't get a full understanding of worldly knowledge, not to mention Buddhism.

Every time when I read a Buddhist book, I often remind myself, "There must be something I can learn from this book." Therefore, I read fairly attentively. Even if I only read a very small paragraph, I ponder repeatedly, "Why was it said in this way?" If we read absentmindedly, it's impossible to savor their excellence.

To understand Buddhism comprehensively, my suggestions are: First, in order to understand Mahayana Buddhism, study the *Guide to the Bodhisattva's Way of Life*. To understand the emptiness of the Mahayana Perfection of Transcendental Wisdom tradition, study the *Fundamental Wisdom of the Middle Way* or the *Introduction to the Middle Way*. To study the stages of practices in Tibetan Buddhism, study the *Great Treatise on the Stages of the Path to Enlightenment* and the *Words of My Perfect Teacher*.

If you study these texts, in the long run, I believe that your body and mind will undergo great transformation.

Can prayers dedicated to victims really dispel their suffering?
It's incorrect to assume it doesn't work at all, but we also
shouldn't say it absolutely works.

It's similar to when patients take medication: the doctor
can't affirm, "This medicine is absolutely effective and can
definitely cure your disease." After all, every patient's situation is different, so the curability is also case by case. Nonetheless, in general, taking medication often has some effect.

Similarly, in order to dispel disaster and suffering, prayers
and Buddhist rituals do help greatly. However, if the karma
is too grave, dedicating prayers may not have any obvious
effect.

Even if this is the case, should we still say prayers? Yes, just
like we take medication when we're sick.

Lecture at Lanzhou University of Finance and Economics
July 3, 2012

9. HAPPINESS IS ROOTED IN THE HEART

Happiness isn't rooted in how much you own, but in how much desire you let go. Socrates once laughed heartily in a market and said, "What a lot of things I don't need!"

NOT LONG AGO, a journalist from the Chinese Central TV interviewed people all across China with the same question, "Are you happy?," and got all sorts of strange answers. Following this trend, a journalist also asked Mo Yan, the Nobel laureate, "Are you happy?" He answered frankly, "I don't know." Afterward he explained, "Happiness is to think about nothing, let go of everything, be healthy, and have no pressure. Right now, I'm extremely stressed and anxious, so how can I be happy? However, if I answered that I'm unhappy, you would say: 'Come on! How can you not be happy after you just won the Nobel Prize?'"

In the eyes of ordinary people, the Nobel Prize makes you rich, famous, and high in social status, and so they think this person must be happy. And yet Mo Yan's answer was "I don't know." Reflecting on this, we can easily understand today's topic: "Happiness Is Rooted in the Heart." In other words, happiness doesn't rely on the external world. Of course, happiness isn't totally unrelated to external objects, but mainly it's up to our hearts.

Poor people do feel happy when they get some money, but once basic living requirements are met, the increase in wealth doesn't necessarily enhance happiness. There was a study a few years ago that put the limit on increased happiness and comfort gained by wealth at an average of $75,000 per year (the precise number in fact differed by state and country). This is to say that if you earn under $75,000 a year, you feel the lack of resources and are less happy. By contrast, earning more than that no longer added to any sense of well-being. For instance, you may feel very happy when you purchase your first house, but when you get the second and the third house, even if they're in exciting locations, the feeling of happiness becomes less distinct.

Many people daydream, "If I had an enormous pile of money, all my problems would be solved, and I would be absolutely happy." The fact is that it's not that easy. Elizabeth Taylor said that in her life, she had possessed wealth, fame, success, and charm, but never happiness.

Wealth sometimes brings suffering instead of happiness. For instance, when you move from a single-story cottage to a high-rise apartment, your property management fees increase. When you trade in your Volkswagen Santana for a brand-new BMW, maintenance fees also go up. Additional afflictive emotions come with all sorts of extra bills.

Buddhism teaches that wealth is inseparable from suffering. In the beginning, there's the suffering of collecting wealth, which comes from working hard. In the middle, there's the suffering of guarding wealth, which comes with worrying about its depreciation or theft. In the end, there's the suffering of losing wealth, which comes when it's devoured by impermanence. Thus, a well-known saying goes, "80 percent of happiness has nothing to do with money, while 80 percent of suffering is closely associated with money."

Having realized that wealth didn't bring him the expected happiness but only suffering, an Austrian millionaire donated all his money to a charitable organization and then moved into a small cabin to live as an ordinary person.

It's impossible to survive in this world without even a penny, but if we have too much money, it also doesn't necessarily make us happy. It's a shame that most people don't understand this, but only blindly wish to make more money. As a result, they go astray from their true aim of being happy.

This circumstance is in large part due to modern education, which emphasizes materialism excessively and rarely mentions the spirit. If personal success or collective development requires more than material improvement and especially if moral degeneration is the cost, we definitely lose more than we gain.

Can power and status guarantee happiness?

Power and position are unreliable also. It's unwise to expect happiness from them.

Countless illustrious people have appeared in history. When they were exalted, they were surrounded by people all the time. With just one word, hundreds of people would come running. But once they left power, even their close relatives and friends didn't call on them. Just like a big tree, when it's branchy and leafy, hundreds of birds gather on it, but when the leaves and branches have withered and fallen, they all fly away.

The hypocrisy of the world repeats itself again and again, but how many people are willing to see through it?

Wise people understand that the higher the position, the greater the pressure. In the *Song of Renunciation*, Emperor Shunzhi laments, "I should have been a monk of the west, so why was I born in the royal family? Deprived of freedom for eighteen years, when will I stop warring in all directions?"

However, worldly people can't resist their attachment to status and are always afraid it will be taken from them. For example, in one anecdote, Hui Shi, Zhuangzi's close friend from childhood, was in a high position in the Liang Kingdom. One time Zhuangzi went to visit him. Thinking that Zhuangzi wanted an official position, Hui Shi was afraid this would threaten his own position because Zhuangzi surpassed him in both wisdom and moral conduct. Having read his mind, Zhuangzi said that he viewed official positions as "rotten rats" and wouldn't even take a look at it, let alone take any interest in it.[12]

Too many people are obsessed with power and status just like Hui Shi. From the Buddhist point of view, it's just not feasible to gain happiness through status. Why? The nature of cyclic existence is suffering, so no matter how hard we exert ourselves, suffering is still the only thing that we can get.

In the *Four Hundred Stanzas on the Middle Way*, the ancient Indian scholar Aryadeva states, "The superior suffer mentally, the inferior ache physically. Because of these two kinds of suffering, worldly beings are tormented every single day."

"The superior" refers to people with high status, fame, and wealth. They don't suffer physically but have indescribable mental pain and all sorts of worries every day. Some of them even toss about in bed every night and have to take sleeping pills to live normally.

"The inferior" means people living at the bottom of society with no status, fame, or money. They generally suffer physically from starvation, fatigue, and having to struggle to survive.

Suffering from power and position falls into the suffering of "the superior." Ponder this: However high the position, it can only last for several decades, so is it worth giving your whole life to it? Buddhism teaches, "Leaving loss and gain to conditions, the mind has no increase or decrease." So, let go of power and position, and avoid mental fluctuation for trivial loss and gain.

Wealth and status are temporary. Whether it's useful or not depends on how you utilize them. If fortunate people use them appropriately, they'll have more opportunity to be happy.

For instance, if I'm rich and in a high position, I can help others with these resources. I can bring happiness to myself and others. If I use my resources to engage in inappropriate business, however, misfortune is bound to arrive. Then it would be better if I didn't have such merit.

Whether worldly merit is useful or not depends on what it can bring about.

Can love guarantee happiness?

Others expect to gain happiness from romantic love. This is even worse. In fact, it's wrong to expect happiness from romantic love. Of course, it's undeniable that it can bring people happiness to some extent.

We should be the master of our own mind; if our happiness is dependent on others, we're bound to be greatly disappointed.

Buddhadharma is inseparable from the secular world. Even the Buddha acknowledged worldly affections. Nonetheless, we have to ponder the way it exists and its related ideas.

Sometimes love becomes a source of suffering instead of happiness. When desire and attachment arise, we're afraid to lose what we're attached to, so fear and worry haunt our mind. Just as it's stated in the *Nirvana Sutra*, "Because of love, there is worry. Because of love, there is fear. When apart from love, where is worry, where is fear?"

For some people, when their relationship goes sour, they can't let it go and they suffer in agony. This is actually just a reflection of their attachment.

Many young people suffer because of love. Their main priority in life is to find their Mr. or Ms. Right, and they crazily fall in love with each other. If they fall out of love for whatever reason, some lose the courage to live and even choose to commit suicide.

This extreme attachment to romantic love is influenced by mass media. In films, TV shows, or literature, love is an inevitable topic and praised as incomparable all the time. Immersed in such an atmosphere, how can people avoid being sucked deeper and deeper into the whirlpool of affection?

Analyzing with wisdom, you'll find that the essence of you, the one you fall in love with, and the relationship between you two is emptiness. With such realization, you'll still have illusory and dream-like romantic love, but you won't cling to it too much.

In fact, love is only a small part of life. It's not everything. There's no need to regard it as too important. Otherwise, if you place your happiness on the person whom you fall in love with, then any change of his or her attitude toward you can cause your happiness to decease dramatically. Such a life is too exhausting, too miserable, and simply not worth it.

Where is happiness?

From childhood to the present, we've learned that happiness comes entirely from outside. However, everything external is unstable and can change at any moment. The happiness revealed in Buddhism can only be established in the heart. Only by recognizing this can we understand what everlasting happiness is.

It's a shame that the majority of people don't know this. Due to their confusion over the cause of happiness, the more they pursue it, the greater their suffering. Some research has shown that China ranks number one in the world in terms of the pressure faced by office workers and the number of deaths that result from overwork. Some other statistics suggest that among every ten Chinese people, there's one case of mental disorder.

What causes this? The main reason is that our minds are untamed. Without contentment, when others have something nice, we immediately feel a desire to own one too. We don't need it; we just want it. Every time when I see people bustling and hustling around in metropolises, I can't help but wonder if such a lifestyle really brings them happiness.

Elvis Presley once desperately lamented that though he had tried everything, he still didn't feel content. The German philosopher Schopenhauer said, "Wealth is like ocean water: the more you drink, the thirstier you are." As one Buddhist sutra points out, "When various desires cannot be satisfied, annoyance and affliction arise." Thus, our suffering is in direct proportion to our desire. To be free from suffering, we must subdue desire.

The weaker the desire, the greater the happiness.

A while ago, a journalist asked me on Weibo, "Are you happy?" I said, "Happy." He added, "Why?" I replied, "Because I feel content."

In order to attain happiness, the key is to understand how to be happy instead of just talking about it and drawing everyone's attention to it. It isn't enough for a patient to realize that he's sick; he has to see a skillful doctor, find out the cause of his disease, and take his medication regularly.

Contentment is the prescription for attaining happiness. When you're content, no matter how plain your life is, you'll still savor happiness.

I read a book recently called *The Private World of Tasha Tudor*. The story was about a grandmother named Tasha who lived on a ranch.

She took great care of her garden and fed various small animals with compassion. She also spun cotton into yarn, wove cloth, and sewed clothes by herself. She lived a simple, idyllic life. Her happiness was envied by countless people.

In my hometown, there's a practitioner who years ago built a thatched cottage deep in the mountains. Every day he chants prayers and meditates all day long. He only has simple food and a few changes of clothes. There's no need to worry about being robbed since he's never once locked the door in over twenty years of living there. Once I went to visit him and I was immediately enchanted— blue sky and white clouds above, green and lush woods all around, a murmuring brook nearby, birds singing, and the fragrance of flowers everywhere—a feeling of being free from the turmoil of the world arose, and all my afflictive emotions vanished without a trace.

Such happiness might appear remote, but if we understand how to feel content, then we can have it right at this very moment. Master Lian Chi said, "Once we understand contentment, all afflictive emotions can be eliminated." A Buddhist sutra also states, "Little desire and inaction bring comfort and ease of body and mind."

In contrast, if you're not content with your current situation, then everything can be a source of suffering. For instance, if you earn $2,000 per month and find out a colleague makes $3,000 every month, you become irritated, saying, "How can he earn more than I do? This shouldn't happen; I'll make more than him!" When the thought of competition arises, suffering immediately follows you like a shadow.

Religious belief can bring happiness.

There are many methods for living happily. Finding happiness through religion is one proven way.

A report indicated that religious believers have a higher happiness index than nonbelievers. A Gallup poll made using 676,000 telephone interviews on the relationship between happiness and religious belief across America from January 2010 to December 2011 showed that the happiness score of religious believers is 69.2, while that of nonbelievers is 65.3.

When facing frustrations, religious believers can move on from them much more easily. A Buddhist once frankly told me, "Due to different misfortunes, I was excruciatingly miserable for a long time, and I even thought of committing suicide more than once. Luckily, I encountered the Buddhadharma, so I was able to shake off that miserable feeling. Otherwise, I can't imagine that I would still be alive."

I'm not intentionally advertising Buddhism, but Buddhism does in fact have a great impact on enhancing happiness.

Take Bhutan for example. The entire nation follows Tibetan Buddhism and is often named one of the happiest countries on earth. In 2008, for instance, an American journalist wrote a book called *The Geography of Bliss* in which he discusses ten of the happiest countries, and Bhutan is one of them.

I have some experience of life in Bhutan. In 1990, Kyabjé Jigme Phuntsok Rinpoché was invited by the King of Bhutan to teach Dharma there. I accompanied him and stayed for half a month. I was impressed that although it's not a rich country—there are few cars or airplanes, for example—everyone seems content and overflowing with happiness. I also remember that in Bhutan there are short poems with profound meaning everywhere. One of them read: "Only when the last tree is cut down, the last river is sucked dry, and the last fish is fished out, can human beings realize, 'Oh, money is inedible.'" This concise poem reflects perfectly the attitude of the Bhutanese, who resist damaging nature and are rethinking human behavior.

On the Qinghai-Tibet Plateau, where Tibetan Buddhism flourishes, people's sense of happiness is also very strong. If it were measured, their happiness index wouldn't be lower than the Bhutanese. In this land, the most remote, and also closest to the sky, the old and young alike overflow with inner contentment, always wearing radiant smiles on their faces.

On the contrary, many urban people suffer indescribable distress even though their material resources are abundant. For them, I recommend they look to the methods of mind training used in traditional Buddhist cultures. When time allows, get out of the city, witness the life of practitioners, and try to appreciate another attitude toward life. Without jumping out of their narrow circle, urban people can only continue to repeat past thinking patterns again and again. Eventually, extreme boredom arises and such people can even become completely lost in their lives. If one adopts a new perspective, however, new realizations may come.

There are numerous approaches to mind training in Buddhism, though meditation has been widely favored in recent years. More than ten thousand Americans rely on it to enhance their quality of life; many universities and corporations have their own meditation centers. When you're suffering and stressed, it doesn't hurt to try it. If you can meditate for a few minutes each day, you'll feel different.

It's almost impossible to avoid being busy in this modern age. If you blindly keep yourself busy to the point of exhaustion and illness, however, you lose more than you gain. I highly agree with ancient people's lifestyle: eat when it's the time to eat, work when it's the time to work, sleep when it's the time to sleep. A simple yet regular life.

Many people with extremely tight schedules dedicate what little spare time they have to their mobile phones. While walking, driving, working, or even partying, they're constantly looking at their cellphones, thus making themselves even busier with trivial things. The first thing they do after waking up in the morning is check their cellphone, and this is also the last thing they do before going to bed at night. Perhaps on their deathbed the thing that will be the most difficult to let go of will be their cellphone.

We don't only live for just one lifetime. Rather than look for present enjoyment, it makes more sense to pursue everlasting happiness. Many people believe that when we die it's just like a fire that goes out without any remainder. This is mistaken. Death is the end of this life, but it's also the beginning of endless future lives. Unfortunately, these days the majority of people are unaware of this. It never occurs to them to ask where they come from at birth and where they'll go after death.

The Buddha taught that during our endless rebirths in cyclic existence, our body disappears but our consciousness does not. Only when we understand this, will we plan for our future. Otherwise, if we assume that life will only last a few more decades, then the most we can attain is some kind of success for a few years.

Q&A

When someone reaches the state where they "give rise to a thought without any clinging," does he or she still need to be mindful of the law of karmic cause and effect?
The statement "give rise to a thought without any clinging" is from the *Diamond Sutra*. It means don't cling to anything and abide in the luminous nature of mind. The Sixth Patriarch attained enlightenment when he heard this line.

The nature of all phenomena is emptiness, but conventional appearance has form. Just like dreaming, the dream is illusory, but you can still experience suffering and happiness.

Therefore, we still have to emphasize the importance of the law of karmic cause and effect, abandoning nonvirtue and adopting virtue. Otherwise, negative actions will accumulate vicious seeds on the all-encompassing foundation (or *alaya*) consciousness. These seeds may ripen in this life or future lives and will bring us suffering sooner or later. In reality, incurable disease or unchangeable fate are the result of past negative karma.

Fortunate people with great wealth and high status always feel unhappy, while some ordinary people feel happier. If this is the case, aren't wealth and status useless?
Wealth and status are the temporary results of merit. Whether they're useful or not depends on how you utilize them. If fortunate people use them appropriately, they'll have greater opportunity to be happy.

For instance, if I'm rich and in a social position, I can help others by using my resources. Thus, I can bring happiness to myself and others. If I use them to engage in inappropriate business, however, misfortune is bound to arrive, and then it would be better if I didn't have this worldly merit. So, whether this merit is useful or not depends on what it can bring about.

How can we encourage others to believe in reincarnation?
If they don't believe in it, ask them to give some convincing reasons. If they can only say, "I don't believe in it because I don't agree with it," this isn't an adequate reason.

How do we know that future lives exist?
Recently, many books about reincarnation have been published. Reading these books can help nonbelievers

understand how reincarnation works. In fact, reincarnation isn't a concept confined to Buddhism. It's acknowledged in many religions and even by nonbelievers. A great portion of the people who can remember their past lives don't follow any religion.

Some people may wonder, "If past lives exist, why can't I remember any?"

This is because when sentient beings enter the womb, the womb obscuration forces memories of past lives to fade, except in the case of very few individuals. Apart from past lives, we forget most of our childhood experiences as well. Still, we can't say that our past lives don't exist only because we can't remember them.

To deny the existence of past and future lives, you must have evidence. I've paid close attention to this topic for over twenty years. Relying on data from ancient times as well as information from more recent studies here and abroad, I've become convinced that past and future lives must exist. I've found no evidence to refute it. This is a truth of life and not a matter of whether you believe it or not.

What's the relationship between cyclic existence and mind?
From the Buddhist point of view, cyclic existence is comprised of six realms. The three higher realms are the god, human, and asura realms; the three lower realms are the realms of hell beings, hungry ghosts, and animals. If one commits negative actions in this life, one will fall into lower realms in future lives. If one performs positive actions in this life, one will be born in the higher realms in future lives. If one practices the supramundane virtues, one can transcend cyclic existence.

The principal characteristic of cyclic existence is mind. This mind is driven by the forces of karma from beginningless time, fluctuating in various life forms in the six realms. Due to different past-life experiences, sentient beings carry distinct habitual tendencies. Take twins as an example: they inherit the same genetic information from their parents, live in the same family, and have a similar education, but due to their different karmic causes and conditions, one may be virtuous and the other may be vicious, and their habitual tendencies, strengths, and abilities may be worlds apart.

To analyze this further, according to the theories of the third turning of the wheel of Dharma in Buddhism, this mind has an attribute of clarity, which will transform into the Buddha's wisdom when one reaches Buddhahood. However, at the stage of ordinary beings, this clarity is covered by various afflictive emotions. Just like gold in a gold mine, at first it's mixed with other elements such as dirt and mud. Yet through repeated refinement, it becomes pure gold.

For us, it's crucial to master the mystery of the mind. If we can recognize the true face of the mind, we won't be attached to any external phenomena. We can then always look at the bright side of things and have the confidence to deal with any problem.

What's your opinion of Chinese national culture, such as the Standards for Being a Good Pupil and Child *and the* Three Character Classic?[13]

As a Tibetan, I received Buddhist education in Tibet from childhood, so I didn't learn about Chinese national culture at that time. When I read these texts later on, I was surprised at how excellent these theories are. I strongly feel young people should study them. Only if they study these can our society have hope. Otherwise, if morality completely degenerates, then no matter how advanced our material development, it will still be meaningless. It's a shame if the *Standards for Being a Good Pupil and Child*, the *Three Character Classic*, the *Analects of Confucius*, and the sacred texts of Daoism aren't studied.

The ten-year Cultural Revolution was a catastrophe that ruined the roots of traditional culture and caused horrific harm to generation after generation. How do we restore traditional culture? On the one hand, the Education Department must call on the public to work toward restoring this cultural legacy. On the other hand, everyone also has a responsibility to study and propagate it on their own. Only in this way can the situation turn around and our society be improved from its root.

Of course, merely discussing it won't bring about change. We must take action. Even if you can't do something major, at least you can start by promoting the *Standards for Being a Good Pupil and Child*. It's straightforward and easy to understand. If you can't find a student to discuss it with, you can teach your children first.

This is a commercialized age. Films, internet, and arts all encourage desire and lust. In such circumstances, is the role of Buddhism very limited?
Buddhism isn't asceticism. In general, Buddhism doesn't demand that you eliminate all your desire. Rather, it reminds you not to be insatiable. This reminder is very important. Buddhism is like a driving coach sitting next to you in the

car; if you forget to brake in time, your Buddhist practice can remind for you.

Current mass media gives unhealthy guidance and has an enormous impact on people's values. At this point, reminders about Buddhist concepts are even more necessary. Otherwise, people may helplessly sink into the depths of desire.

As a Buddhist, I'm willing to give lectures whenever I'm invited, even if the size of the audience is extremely small. Why? Because modern society really needs Buddhist theories. Many people are spiritually barren and have extremely strong desire. So, there must be someone to remind them, "Don't let your desire go too far. Otherwise, you'll suffer greatly."

Of course, Buddhism doesn't ask you to give up making money or to leave all your friends and relatives behind to become monastics and live in the mountains. Even Buddha Shakyamuni didn't emphasize this. The Buddha only told us that lay practitioners should behave their way and monastics should act their way. No matter what identity you have, you all need appropriate spiritual guidance.

I really like meat, but it requires the killing of animals. Should I change my diet?
Even from the point of view of health, a vegetarian diet is good for you. Researchers also find that a vegetarian diet is more suitable to the physiological structure of human beings. If we eat meat, the viruses carried by animals are very likely to infect us, not to mention other negative effects.

If you can't abstain from eating meat, at least don't ask people to kill particular animals for your consumption. Unfortunately, influenced by wrong views, many people assume that animals are just food for human beings. They're unaware that animals also fear death and wish for a long life.

Besides, eating meat is an indirect form of killing animals. You may feel satisfied by gorging on meat in this life, but it's very hard to say what you'll become in future lives. People who are ignorant of the law of karmic cause and effect may feel this is ridiculous. Unfortunately, because of karma, ridiculous things often become a cruel reality.

Many people are interested in fortunetelling. Predicting your life with the year, date, and time of your birth, changing your name, and supplementing the five elements according to fortunetelling are all very popular. It's said that this way a person's fate can be changed. What do you think about this?
Buddhism also includes fortunetelling, divination, and Feng Shui. Predicting things with specific methods has some degree of rationality. Among the various divinatory methods in this world, some of them are authentic and some aren't. Some are legitimate; some are fake. The key is to choose the correct one.

Obviously, even if you find a correct method, don't obsess over it. Although there are rules to divination, our fate isn't unalterable. If we put our energy into cultivating wisdom, compassion, and faith, even without divination, our fate will move toward a better direction. Thus, we should work more on cultivating these virtues.

Mr. Nan Huaijin[14] *just passed away. What do you think of his activities in service of propagating the Dharma?*
The Elder Nan devoted his entire life to propagating the traditions of Buddhism, Confucianism, and Daoism, so I

rejoice in his work and respect him from the depth of my heart. I had a couple opportunities to visit him, but unluckily, I missed him. When I learned of his entering final nirvana, I said prayers for him with other people.

I've read his books. He's really a learned master. What's more precious is that even in his nineties, he was still tirelessly teaching. It's very rare to find such a great master these days.

In regard to reviving traditional culture, we must give the greatest credit to Elder Nan. In the 1990s, traditional culture was just making a comeback, and his books, including *The Diamond Sutra Explained*, became all the rage at the time. Many people used them to refresh their understanding of Buddhism.

Now, Elder Nan has left, but his works remain in the world, so don't be too sad.

Of course, some individuals think of Elder Nan differently. This is normal. From ancient times, when someone becomes famous, there are always widespread rumors about them. This isn't surprising.

How does one begin to study the Middle Way? Would you please introduce the stages for the study and practice of it?
You can start with the *Fundamental Wisdom of the Middle Way*, the *Introduction to the Middle Way*, and the *Four Hundred Stanzas on the Middle Way*.

In the process of studying and meditating on the Middle Way, one will go through four stages of examining. The first is to examine all phenomena as emptiness. The second is to examine emptiness as the union of appearance and emptiness. Third, examine it as nonfabrication. Finally, examine it as equality.

In order to achieve this, there are two approaches. The first is to directly abide in emptiness just like what's described in the sutra of the Sixth Patriarch. The other is to examine all phenomena as emptiness through intensive analysis and then abide in that state.

My friend is a devout Buddhist, but his life was so full of tribulation that he almost had an emotional breakdown. Later, when he became less devout, his misfortunes also decreased. Why?
Your friend's misfortune isn't due to his faith in the Buddhadharma. In reality, seemingly contradictory phenomena often take place: when committing negative actions, everything goes well; when practicing virtue, unfavorable conditions emerge one after another. This isn't because the law of karmic cause and effect is distorted. Generally speaking, when one practices virtue diligently, the future effects of negative karma can ripen in advance, so unfavorable things happen at that time. Once they withdraw from their virtuous practice, life may appear to become more peaceful, but this isn't worth celebrating, because the negative karma isn't exhausted, it's just waiting in the future.

Karma is very complex; we can only understand it through systematic Dharma study.

What's your life mission?
I first thought my life mission was reading, because from elementary school until normal school, what I enjoyed most was reading books. However, after I took ordination, my mind changed. Now I feel that as long as I can, I should share what I've read and my experience of practice from all these years with others.

"Khenpo" is a title that means to pass on knowledge to others. Since I have this title, I should spread the truth I've acquired to all sentient beings. Even if it were my last breath, even if there were only one sentient being, I would do my utmost. This should be my mission.

In fact, everyone should have his or her own mission. Even if we can't make a great difference, as long as we can avoid harming sentient beings and exert ourselves to benefit others or try to do one act of random kindness every day, it's also very meaningful.

Of course, you have to think about it and make your own decision. I can't choose for you. Besides, you might not agree with me!

Lecture at Shanghai Jiao Tong University
October 24, 2012

10. How to Face Suffering

When a doctor prescribes medicine to treat your disease, if you only memorize the prescription without taking the medication, it's obvious that you won't be cured. Similarly, when some people demonstrate for you a brighter approach to living, if you only learn it by heart without taking action, it's apparent that your suffering can't be dispelled.

"Suffering" is not an unfamiliar word to any of us.

It's inappropriate for me to brag about how I removed myself from suffering, since I myself haven't yet completely done so. However, due to my interest in Buddhism since childhood and years of study and practice of Buddhism under the guidance of my spiritual teacher, to some extent I'm able to give a brief report of my own experience.

With money, you suffer; without it, you still suffer.

In the six realms of the three worlds, the different types of suffering are numerous. In the human realm alone there are three types of fundamental suffering and eight kinds of secondary suffering.

The Indian scholar Aryadeva also classified human suffering into two categories: physical suffering and mental suffering. People of high status suffer mentally, experiencing stress, competition, and anxiety in their work. Those in less significant positions suffer physically, lacking basic necessities like sufficient food and clothing and enduring intense workdays.

Many people hold the view that once they have money, they'll be happy. But when they manage to earn a large amount of money, they only find that happiness doesn't arrive as expected. Instead, distress visits them endlessly from then on.

Based on a survey by Gallup in the United States, on a scale of 100 points, the happiness index of Chinese customers was 69 in 1994, reached its peak of 71 in 1997, and fell back to 67 a decade later in 2004.

What does this indicate? With the development of the economy, people first felt increased happiness. But not long after, the happiness index decreased, and people felt even less happy than when the economy was weaker. In 2007, the Beijing Suicide Research and Prevention Center released a report entitled "Suicide Status and Countermeasures in China." The data in this report showed that 287,000 people died by suicide and two million people attempted suicide in mainland China annually. This means that every two minutes, one person died by suicide.

As we can see, many people appear attractive and happy, but inside they feel tortured all the time.

"Why claim that life is full of suffering? I'm quite happy."

There's more suffering than happiness in this world. If you don't believe this, I recommend that you read the first through eighth chapters of the *Four Hundred Stanzas on the Middle Way*, which elaborate the sufferings of human life well and truly. After reading it, you'll understand that suffering is everywhere in human life. As stated in the *Lotus Sutra*, "The three realms are as unsafe as a burning house."

Some people may disagree and ask, "Why claim that life is full of suffering? I'm quite happy." An alcoholic once told me, "Buddhism talks about suffering in samsara. Actually, it's not suffering. I feel extremely cozy after drinking." However, this comfortable feeling that he experiences while drunken is artificial and can't be counted as happiness at all.

The American historian Darrin M. McMahon wrote a book entitled *Happiness: A History*. It took six years of research to investigate what happiness is and what brings it about. He came to the conclusion that ultimate happiness may only be our imagination. In other words, genuine happiness is unattainable. This perspective happens to match the Buddhist view that the three realms offer no lasting peace.

We must remain aware that human life is full of suffering. Otherwise, not understanding that the nature of samsara is suffering, we would readily complain when facing adversity, asking, "Why am I so unlucky? All sorts of misfortune befall me."

Some people say, "Not every aspect of samsara is suffering. There is also some happiness." This sounds reasonable, but the happiness they're referring to is impermanent and may transform into suffering at any moment. Happiness tints our life, but it's not the primary hue.

Others believe that happiness arises from sensory experience: physical touch and melodious music and so forth can all bring happiness. However, such happiness is superficial, and it can also be obtained using drugs.

Genuine happiness comes from your mind. If you wish to dispel suffering, start working on your mind.

How do worldly people handle suffering?

Some people who suffer desperately smoke or drink.

Once a Buddhist told me that it's impossible for him to quit smoking and drinking. Whenever he feels restless, he hides himself in a coffee shop to suck on a cigarette or drowns his sorrows in a bar. He told me that all his problems are solved when he's intoxicated. But can this be true? This must only make him worry more. When sobering up, he still has to face all the problems waiting for him. There's nowhere to hide.

When in a bad mood, some people either indulge in sensual pleasures, shout in a karaoke bar, or stay up playing mahjong. These are all methods of escape.

Some people describe their suffering on a piece of paper and then burn it. Seeing the writing vanish in a puff of smoke, they imagine their suffering also disappearing. This is sort of self-deceiving.

Others go to scream in a valley, knock their heads against a wall, or smash kitchen utensils. They only feel relieved by venting in these ways.

Even worse, some people amuse themselves by killing. Once I read a story about a seventeen-year-old American boy who killed his parents, and while the corpses were still in the house, invited several dozen friends through Facebook to join him for a drinking bash that lasted all night.

After a breakup, some people commit suicide and some kill their lovers. If the lover's whereabouts are unknown, a similar person might become the target. There's a widespread belief on Chinese college campuses that there is a male student who kills female students who wear red clothes and have middle-length hair in order to retaliate against his ex-girlfriend.

People with better coping skills may choose to travel, chat with wise people, go for a psychological consultation, or read some inspirational books like *Chicken Soup for the Soul*. But these approaches, like painkillers, can only temporarily suppress suffering; they only treat the symptoms and not the root cause. To uproot suffering, one should search for solutions in Buddhist traditions.

Here are some Buddhist methods for dispelling suffering.

Even though some habitual tendencies are so ingrained in us that they can't be removed immediately, as long as we keep trying, suffering will gradually decrease. Here are some practices you can choose from.

1. Benefit others, stop being selfish

At times when we've felt such anguish that it's been hard to go on living, we've felt this way on account of our own problems, not because of the problems faced by others. To dispel suffering, we must cut it off at its source—the selfish mind. In order to achieve this, we must study Buddhist sutras and commentaries. These can help us transform our attitude in accordance with Mahayana Buddhism's view of selflessness.

Some people used to suffer from a variety of afflictions, yet after they began to study Dharma, they engaged in activities for the benefit of others, and their suffering disappeared without a trace. Therefore, the first method of dispelling suffering is to benefit others.

It would be fantastic if you had compassion and the awakened mind of the Mahayana tradition, but if you don't have these, at least try to cultivate benevolence. It's one of the best forms of medicine for improving human society.

Education systems needs to improve. High test scores aren't good enough. Currently, college entrance exam scores are basically the only criterion for college admission. In reality, a student's scores aren't so important; his or her character is key. Some people are quite smart, but if their character is awful, they won't make positive contributions and instead will do tremendous harm to society.

The most important dimension of education is teaching students to be good people. In old times, evaluating whether a person should be promoted to an important position was done based not only on their knowledge, but also their moral conduct. If a person is noble and trusted by the public, even if they aren't so knowledgeable, they can still take an important position. On the contrary, without a compassionate and kind heart, even if their knowledge overflows, it's impossible for them to make people in their country and the world happy.

I heard that at the headquarters of the United Nations in New York, there's a mosaic of the biblical "Golden Rule": "Do unto others as you would have them do unto you." This is exactly as Confucius said, "What you do not want, do not give to others." It's a shame that while many people know this saying, very few apply it. When our lives are endangered, we're afraid of death and seek survival, but not many people have the empathy to realize that the animals slaughtered for our dinner table feel exactly the same fear.

When giving up selfishness, benefiting sentient beings can't just be lip service. We have to engage in a multidimensional analysis in order to determine if we can fulfill this aim. If we can, we're bound to become free from suffering.

2. Transform adversity into favorable conditions

To deal with adversity, Buddhism has another approach: turn it into the path. In other words, don't treat suffering as suffering, but instead make use of it.

Thogmé Sangpo's *Song of Happiness* reads: When I'm ill, I'm happy, because karmic obscurations can be eliminated through illness. When I'm healthy, I'm still happy, because a healthy body can be used to do virtuous deeds. When I'm rich, I'm happy, because I can make offerings to the worthy and give alms to the poor. When I'm poor, I'm still happy, because it helps me to get rid of attachment to money and material goods.

In regard to this, one of my middle school classmates is an excellent example. He's a government officer. Once, before an election to a higher position, he showed no sign of concern for it but treated it as if it had nothing to do with him. Other people were anxious for him and advised him to launch a campaign. He smiled and said, "In case I'm not elected, it's quite good to have more time for Dharma practice; if I'm elected, then I have greater opportunity to serve sentient beings. Whatever the result is, I'm happy either way."

However, it's a shame that the majority of people don't understand this. They worry about their personal gain and loss and complain about whatever happens. As a result, even favorable conditions become adversity. If they could change the way they look at the world, even adversity could become favorable.

Romain Rolland, in his book on Beethoven, called him a great man for taking his own suffering and transforming it into a source of happiness for others, saying "the darkness of the world is made clear by the guiding light" of such heroes.

3. Practice the exchange of self and other

Whether you're sick in bed, your reputation suffers, or you're bankrupt, you can make this aspiration: "So many people in this world suffer exactly the same way I do; may their misfortune be transferred to me. I'm willing to take this on so that they can be happy, free from suffering."

When you inhale, visualize their suffering in the form of black smoke dissolving into you. When you exhale, visualize your happiness being offered to sentient beings in the form of white light.

This is the best way to eliminate suffering.

When encountering misfortune, if we practice in this way, our suffering fulfills its value, and our self-clinging will decrease day by day.

4. Recognize that suffering is empty by nature
Suffering comes from conceptual thoughts, which can be eradicated through realizing emptiness. In his *Four Hundred Stanzas on the Middle Way*, Aryadeva states, "The fetter of delusive conceptual thoughts can be removed by realizing the view of emptiness."

Why? The suffering "I" and suffering itself exist interdependently. Without one, the other can't exist. It's also said in the *Fundamental Wisdom of the Middle Way*, "Apart from the object, how can the subjective person exist? Apart from the subjective person, how can the object exist?" Some people make complaints all day long, but where is this suffering "I"? Through scrutinizing it with the right view of the Middle Way, we can understand that "I" doesn't exist at all. If this is true, the suffering "I" is just illusory fabrication.

Without realizing emptiness, one is unable to see through the "I" or let it go, and they take illusion for intrinsic existence. If we can eliminate self-clinging through understanding emptiness just as many great practitioners have done, all sorts of suffering will disappear without residue and the resultant enlightenment will bring indescribable happiness.

Of course, we don't necessarily have that kind of realization, but at least we should have some understanding of the idea that every phenomenon is empty by nature. In order to comprehend this, it's best to start with the *Fundamental Wisdom of the Middle Way*. The opening line of this text reads, "Everything that arises interdependently is unceasing and unborn, neither nonexistent nor everlasting, neither coming nor going, neither several in meaning nor with a single meaning—all concepts and duality are pacified." These few words have thoroughly revealed the truth of all phenomena. Whether it's inner suffering or outer objects, their nature is indeed neither arising nor ceasing, neither everlasting nor nonexistent, neither several in meaning nor with a single meaning, neither coming nor going.

In order to dive into Buddhism, it's necessary to study and practice earnestly step by step. Some people took refuge over a decade ago, but they have only randomly read a couple of books and superficially understood very few Buddhist principles. This doesn't necessarily qualify them as authentic Buddhists.

Nowadays, there are two misunderstandings commonly found among Buddhists.

Firstly, unlike Tibetan practitioners who spend tons of time teaching, debating, composing, studying, reflecting, and meditating on Buddhism, some scholars only study Buddhism academically, thinking that obtaining a master's degree or PhD in Buddhist studies is good enough. Their understanding of Buddhism is superficial and their theses lack true meaning, yet their arrogance steadily grows as time goes by.

Secondly, blindly believing that there's a shortcut to liberation, some believers are quite superstitious, seeking empowerments and blessings everywhere. Even a secular compulsory education requires nine years of study to finish middle school. Given Buddhism is so profound, how can it be mastered in such a short period of time? Without systematic study, if one claims to be Buddhist after obtaining a refuge certificate or an empowerment, it's a false claim.

Once when I conversed with a professor, both of us agreed on this common understanding: in the case of Buddhism, theoretical research isn't enough, actual practice is required. On the contrary, it's unacceptable to blindly practice without theoretical support. Therefore, both theory and practice are essential.

Another time, a university lecturer asked, "I've told Buddhist stories to university students, but they don't believe them. What should I do?"

I said, "No need to tell stories. Having become used to listening to myths and watching cartoons, they naturally relate Buddhist stories to these materials. Start with the Middle Way and Buddhist logic. Only after their arrogance is destroyed will they be able to appreciate the greatness of Buddhism when you tell such stories."

In my lecture at Fudan University, I quoted a remark by the former chancellor of the University of Science and Technology of China: "When scientists finally reach the mountaintop after all kinds of hardship, Buddhist masters will have been waiting for them for a long time." Knowledge in any field can be perfectly interpreted using Buddhist theories. Of course, some people may not have yet become acquainted with Buddhism, but this isn't the fault of Buddhism. It's his or her own issue.

5. Learn to be patient

To be patient means to be forbearing in a conventional sense. When we're forbearing, we won't easily bow to difficulties.

The well-known American writer Helen Keller, who was blind and deaf, created inconceivable miracles over the course of her tough life. Marie Curie also said, "First principle: never to let one's self be beaten down by persons or by events." When Curie was studying in school, she was impoverished and suffered unbearable austerity. Due to malnutrition, she fainted not just a couple of times; lacking bedclothes in cold weather, she had to put on all her clothes and even a chair on top to make her body feel warm.

In Tibetan Buddhism, there was a great patriarch named Longchenpa. When he was meditating at Samye, he only owned a yak-hair sack. When it snowed, he would get into this sack. This very sack was his duvet, meditation cushion, and outerwear.

This reminds me of a small fox featured in a film about animal protection. In the film, the fox says:

"I have a pretty piece of clothing that I wear year-round. For my entire life, I have only had this one piece of clothing, which was given by my mother when I was born. From then on, I have worn it every day and have never taken it off even when I sleep at night.

"Human beings, I have only one piece of clothing, while your closets are overflowing. My clothing is my fur, and once I lose it, I'll become just a glob of blood and flesh. You can change your clothing three times per day, but if my clothes were taken off, I would die and go to the underworld."

If we give up wearing fur, we still have many choices for clothing. If we give up eating meat, we still have many vegetables to eat. For many people, a piece of meat means nothing, but have you ever considered that animals only have this flesh? If you eat it, they have to die for you.

There are many animal protection organizations in the West, but we don't have many here in China. However, it's still good if we can work for animals' benefit. If you have a favorite kind of meat, try to eat less. This is a form of compassion.

6. Recite mantras to lift up one's mood

In Tibetan Buddhism, there's a practice that can help us improve interpersonal relationships, maintain a good mood, and even solve various kinds of problems if we practice it often.

It's very straightforward: set your gaze straight in the space in front of you, completely relax without any attachment, let your mind expand to become as vast as possible, and then abide in this state calmly. Afterward, recite the mantra *tayata om tsomo milena deka tamo svaha* seven or 108 times.

I practiced this for quite a while and found it very effective. Of course, if you don't have faith in it, the effect may not be so obvious. Faith is key for any practice.

Some people may think that this isn't rational. As a matter of fact, both extreme rationality and excessive emotion can prevent you from advancing in profound fields.

Some scholars and researchers reject the concepts of faith and blessing and turn their noses up at these terms. They believe in nothing except for their own conceptual thoughts. However, some people are superstitious and gullible, and they never study any theory. This is another extreme. In order to understand the true nature of this world, we have to take a middle way and avoid these two extremes.

7. Let go of your attachment

Once, an artist painted a black dot on a piece of paper and had it framed. People who had the chance to view it made all kinds of guesses, not knowing its meaning. In fact, the message it delivers is quite profound: when we focus on one thing, we usually neglect many others, completely ignoring the vast space around it.

An acquaintance of mine was facing some issues with her spouse and at times she almost wanted to give up her life. Not knowing what to do, she hired a driver to take her to the great prairie of Ramthang in the Tibetan region. It was particularly vast. They drove for about ten miles and saw no sign of any edges to the grassland. She got out of the car and asked the driver to leave her alone for a while. Then, she started to shout and scream as loudly as possible to air her grievances. While she was shouting and screaming, her mind gradually opened up. Taking a look at the sky, gazing at the grassland, she felt that she was just like a tiny ant desperately clinging to a small nest. How can this be meaningful? She let go of it right away, and her suffering also disappeared.

In the eyes of Buddhist practitioners, suffering isn't a surprise. In the *Guide to the Bodhisattva's Way of Life*, Shantideva states that when the situation is remediable, there's no need to be distressed; if it's not remediable, there's no use being distressed. For instance, when someone you hold close and dear passes away, if you can't revive him or her, then there's no need to be distressed; if reviving the person is impossible, then what will crying do? However, very few people can really think this way.

Of course, I'm not saying that I'm capable of doing this or facing any circumstance calmly. However, by spending a long time studying Mahayana Buddhism, I do have a completely different feeling when seeing family members passing.

Many people share similar experiences: before studying the Dharma, it's very hard to handle things even when very few afflictive emotions arise. However, through Dharma study, most issues in our daily life become resolved, and most people feel happy in most circumstances. None of this can be purchased with money.

If you are an emanation of a buddha or bodhisattva, it's a different matter, but if you're an ordinary person like me, I suggest that you study the Dharma. If you follow this suggestion, your suffering will gradually vanish.

8. Recognize awareness

In my experience, recognizing one's intrinsic awareness is the simplest and most straightforward approach, requiring no analysis of Middle Way theory. Merely relying on a pith instruction from a guru, one can recognize the nature of suffering and transform afflictive emotions into enlightenment at the very moment they arise.

This is also the most profound pith instruction of the Tantrayana.

However, it's worth mentioning that to practice this pith instruction requires empowerment and completion of the preliminary practices. If you're not qualified, you aren't even allowed to read the related texts. Some people stealthily flip through tantric Buddhist texts, but without the instruction and guidance of a guru, even if you understand the words literally, you won't be able to figure out what they really mean.

You don't have to try all of the methods mentioned above. People have different faculties, so it's okay to just choose the one that works best for you, just as a sick person could choose Chinese medicine, Western medicine, or even Tibetan medicine. No matter which one you choose, the purpose is to remove suffering.

Suffering comes from the mind, so it has to be destroyed by the mind. If you want to buy happiness with money, you won't be successful. Only by taming your mind with Buddhadharma can suffering be eradicated from its very root.

Q&A

Modern brain science has found that certain areas of the brain are related to emotion, memory, and so forth. Many people believe that consciousness is a product of the brain. When the brain stops working, consciousness can't exist. Would you please dispel this kind of thinking?

In modern brain science, the examination of the brain is confined to partial structures. So, in regard to the relationship between mind and brain, lots of blanks still remain in scientific circles. So far, even in Carl Jung's psychology, the essence of mind hasn't yet been thoroughly examined. Setting aside the principles revealed in the Tantrayana of the Great Vehicle, most people can't fully understand the relationship between mind and mental events described in the *Abhidharmakosha* of the Basic Vehicle.

It's wrong to say, "When the brain stops working, consciousness disappears." The number of known cases of people who have lived without much of their brain has reached several hundred so far. Also, in the autobiography of the Sixth Dalai Lama, he says that he witnessed a living person without a head and felt that the karma of sentient beings was inconceivable.

Hello Rinpoché, I would like to ask a question for my American friend. Why is transmission so important in Buddhism? Do we still have to emphasize transmission when we have advanced scientific means for recording in this digital age?
Any transmission in Buddhism, including the transmission of the monastic precepts, is of great importance.

In the Tibetan area, we have an intact transmission of the Buddhist canon and commentaries that were produced generation after generation, which is extremely rare. However, we never received the transmission of the precepts for fully ordained nuns. As a result, female monastics can't receive these precepts. But in the Chinese area, this transmission has been preserved up to the present.

What's the use of these transmissions? They work for continuity and blessing. In other words, they continuously pass the blessing of the Buddha on to us, which is essential for practitioners.

It's not only Buddhism that emphasizes transmission or lineage. This is also a common practice in secular settings. Take the presidents of the United States as an example; this is also counted as a lineage. If a mundane lineage is important, a lineage in Buddhism is even more so.

You mentioned that when we're experiencing suffering, we should cultivate compassion by thinking of other people, making aspirations and dedications. This will dispel our own suffering, right?
This depends on the level of every individual's practice.

But what if I still feel pain? Like when I know my guru is sick, I really hope he'll recover immediately.
As it's said in the *Mahayana Uttaratantrashastra*, genuine

noble beings transcend birth, aging, illness, and death, and are free from disease or suffering. However, for the sake of benefiting others, they manifest being sick in the presence of sentient beings.

Therefore, feeling pain for the guru as a disciple is a manifestation of ordinary beings' worry for noble beings.

So a guru manifests as ill for the sake of sentient beings, just like the lay practitioner Vimalakirti?
If the guru is a great accomplisher, the answer is yes. If the guru is an ordinary person, disciples should still care for him or her.

Last year, I invited my guru to hold a Dharma gathering for some of his disciples. Have I done right? What else can I do?
I don't know the specific conditions of your Dharma gathering. However, no matter what kind of Dharma gathering, it's better not to ask participants for money or engage in other inappropriate activities, which isn't good for your guru or Buddhism as a whole.

As Buddhists, we should be responsible for Buddhism, for our guru, and ourselves. If what you're doing may cause some sort of misunderstanding, then stop it. However, if it can really help to spread the Dharma and benefit sentient beings, then spare no effort, even when your life is at risk.

Years ago, in order to protect the Buddhadharma, my guru Jigme Phuntsok Rinpoche calmly faced tremendous danger. As a result, many disciples he trained at that time are strong-minded in regard to spreading the Dharma and benefiting sentient beings. I hope you can follow their examples.

Nowadays, the conditions for Dharma study are so open and free. You should treasure this. Not only should we cultivate genuine faith and the right view, we should also reveal the authentic truths of Buddhism to people around the world. Every Buddhist has this responsibility. We should try to realize this aim.

I follow the Kagyu lineage, so can I register for your online courses? Are there conflicts among different lineages? If I join online study, what are the tantric vows I need to take?
Yes, you can. Our online courses mainly concern the *Guide to the Bodhisattva's Way of Life*, the *Words of My Perfect Teacher*, and so forth, so they don't involve tantric teachings. There's no need to take tantric vows.

All the Tibetan Buddhist lineages, either Kagyu, Sakya, Nyingma, or Geluk, belong to one harmonious system and don't contradict each other. It's said that in Hong Kong, there are disciples from different lineages, including some Dharma centers, who are in conflict. This isn't good. No matter which lineage you follow, they all teach us to generate bodhichitta at the beginning, accumulate merit in the middle, and attain buddhahood in the end. These concepts are all the same; there's no difference.

So, when we study the Dharma, we should be inclusive and open-minded. Even when it comes to non-Buddhist religions, we shouldn't turn away from them but instead seek common ground while accepting differences harmoniously.

Our world is the world of Buddha Shakyamuni. Usually buddha realms are pleasant, but ours is full of suffering. Does this mean that Buddha Shakyamuni didn't make positive aspirations?

No. As described in *White Lotus: Buddha Shakyamuni's Great Biography*, at his causal stage, Buddha Shakyamuni made five hundred great aspirations, and these aspirations are supreme among all the aspirations made by one thousand people who made aspirations at the same event.

Why? All the other people chose pure realms, and only Buddha Shakyamuni chose this impure realm out of his compassion toward miserable sentient beings here.

There's a Buddhist sutra called the *White Lotus Sutra* explaining the white-lotus-like great aspirations, and it comments that the great aspirations made by Buddha Shakyamuni are supreme among those made by other buddhas in this virtuous eon.

Personally, I always reflect on Buddha Shakyamuni's kindness. Had he never made the decision to liberate sentient beings in this impure world, how could we become liberated? We should all be grateful to him.

Do we need to have the wisdom of emptiness to be reborn in the Pure Land of Great Bliss? Do we need to realize emptiness to be born in the Pure Land with unexhausted karma?
It's unnecessary to realize emptiness before one is born in the Pure Land. Relying on the aspirations of the Buddha Amitabha, one can realize emptiness, attain the level of a bodhisattva, and liberate sentient beings after being born in the Pure Land with unexhausted karma.

I've read many books on Buddhist philosophy and have some understanding of the Four Seals. However, when I'm criticized in the workplace, I'm unable to use those principles. How can I avoid being influenced by external settings?

When you're criticized by your boss or colleagues in the workplace, you can treat it like echoes in a valley. This is an instruction in Longchenpa's *Finding Comfort and Ease in the Illusoriness of Things* as well as Venerable Atisha's teachings.

Alternatively, you can treat it as praise. This is also a practice. In the past, when Buddha Shakyamuni was praised or slandered, he treated all these equally without discrimination and wasn't influenced by external circumstances.

I would like to recommend that you study the *Guide to the Bodhisattva's Way of Life*. Even if you don't have time to study the entire text, it would be good if you could manage to study the chapter on patience. If you do, you'll be able to tolerate any suffering or unfairness in the future and live more happily.

Of course, Dharma study can't just be words without actual practice. After you gain mastery over these simple practices, it's safe for you to perform more advanced ones. Nowadays, so many people are doing the opposite. They request the most profound practices first, and only after they find they can't manage them do they engage in basic ones. This is the wrong order, just like doing a PhD program first and then elementary school afterward.

Lecture at the Hong Kong Polytechnic University
July 29, 2011

11. EIGHT SECRETS TO HAPPINESS

Buddhism can make every individual happier. If it doesn't have this effect, we needn't widely spread it nor practice it by ourselves. However, evidence has proven that it does have this impact. At a time when people are so overstressed, it's more important than money.

IN THE TANG dynasty, the empress Wu Zetian wrote a verse: "The most profound, unsurpassable subtle Dharma is so difficult to encounter in hundreds and thousands of millions of eons. Since I get the chance to see, hear, receive, and practice it now, may I understand the ultimate meaning of the Thus Come One." This means that the Buddhadharma is profound and subtle, yet at the same time, the chances of hearing it are extremely rare. Therefore, fortunate ones who have heard it should ensure that they master its meaning.

The secrets of happiness that I'm going to talk about today are from a commentary that's easy to find but difficult to understand. It's called *The Eight Verses of Mind Training*.

This commentary has been around for over eight hundred years. In the ninth century, Tibetan Buddhism was destroyed by King Langdarma. In order to revive Tibetan Buddhism, the succeeding Tibetan king invited Venerable Atisha from India to Tibet. The latter overcame all obstacles to propagate the Dharma. Thereafter, the authentic Mahayana Dharma was revived. One of Venerable

Atisha's disciple's disciples, Langri Thangpa, is the author of this commentary.

The Eight Verses of Mind Training *can bring genuine happiness.*

Thanks to the revival of Buddhism in Tibet, nowadays these eight secrets of happiness can be found everywhere, whether in monasteries, schools, or ordinary people's homes. It appears simple, but its profundity can't be matched.

Right after I took ordination, my guru taught me this. But at that young age, I was relatively arrogant and thought this text was too easy to understand and not extraordinary at all. However, I realized I was wrong as time went on. Over the past thirty years, every time I ruminate on it, I gain different rewards.

When first encountering *The Eight Verses of Mind Training,* you may think, "It's nothing! I could write better verses." But in fact, these lines emanate the wisdom of noble beings, and they're completely different from words assembled by ordinary people. They can bring us genuine happiness.

Happiness requires practical approaches to taming the mind. Only when we master this skill can our sense of happiness increase over time.

The Eight Verses of Mind Training is a secret instruction for happiness. In Tibet, all the great masters emphasize the importance of this work. In Larung Gar, where I reside, each monastic has to memorize three commentaries. This is one of them.

Of course, it's not easy to fully actualize what's described in it. *The Eight Verses of Mind Training* give guidelines for the behavior and actions of noble beings. This isn't true only for householders fettered by mundane pursuits; even we monastics can't fully fulfill what it has advised.

However, although it's not easy, we still need to make great efforts to follow this text. If it's really out of our reach, we should at least make aspirations according to the text and wish to be able to achieve them in the future, or post it in a conspicuous place to constantly remind ourselves.

Some people may ask, "Can such a short text containing only eight secrets be so supreme?" The answer is yes. The blessing of these secrets is inconceivable. In the most concise languages, it reveals the most profound principles, just like a small key could open the gate to a hidden treasure.

To make things more efficient, instead of expounding the text in great detail, I'll just introduce it to you briefly. If this were Tibet, we could spend more time discussing it. There's an old Buddhist teacher in my hometown who's over eighty years old. He usually teaches from one o'clock to seven o'clock nonstop every afternoon. No matter how exhausted the audience feels, he takes his time and teaches slowly. My style is different, so you don't need to worry.

The first secret to happiness: turn loving "me" into loving others.

The root text reads:

> With the intention of benefiting all sentient beings,
> which is more precious than wish-fulfilling jewels,
> may I cherish all sentient beings in cyclic existence
> as dearly as possible at every single moment.

Commentarial note: A mind benefiting others is more precious than a wish-fulfilling jewel. May I care for all sentient beings at every moment with this mind.

Wish-fulfilling jewels can accomplish whatever wish you make before them. Worldly people believe that such jewels are extremely difficult to find, but as a matter of fact, an altruistic heart is even more precious.

What this age most needs is this altruistic mind. If everybody holds on to selfish ideas all the time, society is bound to become less peaceful. Only if we can equally care for all sentient beings without regional, national, or racial discrimination can society be improved.

Years ago, there was a news story about the last game in a public tennis championship. The score had remained the same for a long time between the two sides, and the winner depended on just one shot.

Just at that critical moment, a small bird suddenly flew onto the court. Hit by the high-speed tennis ball, it fell to the ground and died.

The player who killed the bird by mistake gave up his pursuit of winning the game. Disregarding his opponent's shot, he ran to the bird and knelt down immediately in front of it and confessed his fault with his hands joined together at his chest. Hundreds and thousands of spectators were watching him.

Some people didn't understand his choice—was it worthwhile to give up a possible championship just for a dead bird? Of course it was worthwhile. A heart that respects life is more valuable than whatever kind of championship.

From the Buddhist point of view, such a mind can be elevated to meet the essence of the Mahayana Buddhadharma—bodhichitta. It's said in the *Guide to the Bodhisattva's Way of Life*, one would rather give up money, reputation, and even life than withdraw from the bodhichitta that benefits sentient beings.

We need to recognize that all sentient beings have done kind things for us. Putting aside all the things they've done in the past, just look at the present. Our food, clothing, shelter and transportation: which of these doesn't require effort and hardship on the part of other sentient beings? Only if we feel grateful and think more about other sentient beings than ourselves can this make sense. And only in this way can happiness come without invitation.

In fact, one's suffering all stems from loving "me." If we could change loving "me" to "them," our suffering would greatly decrease.

Apart from the views of Buddhism, even modern scientists have discovered that all human beings are derived from the same ancestor based on DNA analysis. So, all human beings on the earth are family members.

If this is the case, why not give up attachment and try loving every single human being?

The second secret to happiness: being respected feels good, but respecting others will make you happier.

Root text:

> When I am in the company of whomever,
> may I regard myself as the lowest among all,
> and from the depths of my heart,
> may I sincerely respect and care for others.

Commentarial note: No matter who I associate with, may I have no arrogance and sincerely think of benefiting them all the time.

In the *Book of Rites* it says, "A courteous man is a man who respects others and lowers himself."[15]

However, many people don't understand the importance of conduct. Whether walking or talking, they always put on a defiant manner. In fact, respecting others is a basic characteristic of human beings. If you don't respect others, you won't be respected either.

Some people can't understand this and say, "I obviously have a higher social status than him, so why should I be humble toward him?" We should understand that everybody has qualities to be respected. Moreover, only when you remain modest while in a high position can you avoid being extremely arrogant and imperious.

The mistake we human beings make most easily is to be arrogant, whether in the context of worldly pursuits or Dharma study. This can hinder our progress in our studies and on the path, and limit our success in whatever we engage.

It's not so great to have a temporary, worldly fortune. Every phenomenon in this world is impermanent; no matter how opulent you may be, you could become homeless overnight. Not long ago, a government official in Guangzhou was exposed for having twenty-two properties. He was deposed immediately, and all his properties were confiscated. Who can guarantee that we won't suffer a miserable turnabout one day? If you really understand impermanence, will you still be able to look down on others?

Many people think they possess certain advantages that give rise to some unintelligible superiority. Nagarjuna said that some people are proud of their talent, some their good looks, some their wealth, and some their high status. If you have a similar attitude, you should read more history to learn about the fates of these kinds of people.

Living in this world, we should learn not only for the sake of accumulating knowledge but also to become a good person. To be a good person isn't to treat people with propriety but to respect them from the depth of one's heart.

Mahayana Buddhism has a very profound explanation on this topic.

The most essential concepts of Mahayana Buddhism are great

compassion, great love, and the awakened mind. Great compassion is the wish to remove suffering from sentient beings; great love is the wish to bring happiness to sentient beings; the awakened mind, or bodhichitta, is the wish that sentient beings attain the long-lasting liberation of buddhahood on top of the former two.

With a virtuous mind, you can respect sentient beings sincerely. This can be seen in the words and acts of many great masters.

Of course, what great practitioners have done is out of reach for us not only for the present lifetime but even for one hundred lifetimes. However, though we can't emulate them 100 percent, it's okay if we can master 20 percent, 10 percent, or even 5 percent of their abilities. We should never give up completely just because we can't be the best.

The third secret to happiness: destroy afflictive emotions just as they begin to arise.

Root text:

> May I constantly watch my mind during daily activities
> so that just when afflictive emotions and thoughts arise
> I can immediately avert them directly and effectively,
> because they can destroy myself and others.

Commentarial note: May I constantly watch my mind, so that every time afflictive emotions and thoughts arise, I can realize that they will destroy myself and others and immediately avert them effectively.

Presently people have fierce afflictive emotions. As it says in the *Kshitigarbha Sutra*, "None of their thoughts and emotions are neither negative karma nor downfalls."

When controlled by afflictive emotions, people easily lose their conscience and commit unimaginable misdeeds.

Browsing online, we can see news like this everywhere: jerry-built building projects, poisons found in baby formula, cooking oil revealed to have been recycled from gutters and sewers. People feel no sense of security while eating meals, drinking water, and walking on the street. The cause of this kind of tragedy is due to the lack of understanding of the law of karmic cause and effect and because their afflictive emotions, such as avarice, are overflowing. Francis Bacon described these kinds of people vividly in "Of Wisdom for a Man's Self": "And certainly it is the nature of extreme self-lovers, as they will set a house on fire, and it were but to roast their eggs."

Driven by afflictive emotions, all sorts of conflicts like wars, fights, quarrels, and tiffs can break out among nations, ethnic groups, families, and friends and colleagues. Once while walking on the street in Shanghai, I saw two vendors fighting for some petty profit. Though it wasn't too violent—they only threw apples at each other—it still counted as a fight.

To destroy afflictive emotions, the best weapon is an altruistic mind. No matter what activities we engage in, if we have the motivation to benefit others and try our best to decrease the idea of cherishing ourselves, then afflictive emotions will be destroyed very soon. Once afflictive emotions are destroyed, suffering won't exist.

The fourth secret to happiness: whoever is miserable must still have some positive qualities.

Root text:

> Whenever I see inferior beings
> suffering intensely due to their misdeeds,

may I cherish them as something rare
as though I were encountering a precious treasure.

Commentarial note: If somebody is suffering now due to their previous misdeeds, may I cherish such a precious opportunity to help these miserable beings as though I have encountered a priceless treasure.

We lack love in the current age. Due to self-concern, many people are unwilling to care about others. During the aforementioned fight between the two vendors, there were many people watching, but nobody even tried to mediate. Although this incident didn't cause severe consequences, essentially it's the same as another story called "the Little Yue Yue Accident," which resulted in the tragic death of a two-year-old girl who had been struck by a car; at least eighteen people walked past her without helping, and the nineteenth passerby stopped and tried to help, but by that time it was too late.

Based on the spirit of the Mahayana, when encountering circumstances like this, including miserable beings who are starving, disabled, or begging, and so forth, what shall we do? We should cherish this opportunity to benefit others as joyfully as though we had discovered a gold mine and do our best to help them.

Many people are generous toward others, but often only when disaster strikes. For instance, during the period of the Wenchuan earthquake, many people had given support to the victims. However, once the calamity was over, it wasn't their business anymore. From the perspective of Mahayana Buddhism, this occasional generosity is far from enough.

In the worst-case scenario, some people remain indifferent when seeing others suffering and don't lift a finger. They think, "Miserable people must have done something negative—they deserve it!" Such an attitude is far removed from the spirit of Mahayana Buddhism.

Of course, it's not easy to transform one's stereotyped preconceptions into the spirit of Mahayana Buddhism in a short time. However, I do hope that in the future, you can at least make some effort to care more about people and things with a virtuous mind.

A virtuous mind needs to be cultivated little by little. Even if you can't make a big commitment, you might try to do one virtuous act a day. Each day, do at least one thing that could benefit yourself and others: when you see someone having difficulty walking, go forward and lend an arm to support him or her; when you're blamed by others, pause and be tolerant; when jealousy arises in your heart, notice it and adjust it immediately. As time goes on, a virtuous mind will surely become a habit.

The fifth secret to happiness: others' slander toward you is the greatest kindness.

Root text:

> When out of jealousy,
> others slander me unreasonably,
> may I take loss and defeat upon myself
> and give the gain and victory to others.

Commentarial note: If somebody slanders me out of jealousy, may I willingly accept the loss and defeat and give the gain and victory to him or her.

This verse has immense blessing.

As recorded in the *Words of My Perfect Teacher*, once, Geshé Chekawa stopped by at Geshé Chakshingwa's place. He saw a small text, opened it, and came across this sentence: "May I take loss and defeat upon myself and give the gain and victory to others." He thought it was so wondrous and asked Chakshingwa immediately, "What's this teaching called?"

Chakshingwa replied, "*The Eight Verses of Mind Training*, by Venerable Langri Thangpa."

Chekawa couldn't wait to receive this teaching, but unfortunately, Venerable Langri Thangpa had already passed away. Afterward, through various hardship, he finally received the transmission of this teaching from Geshé Sharawa. Over the next six years, he practiced this teaching without distraction, and finally achieved supreme realization.

From a worldly person's point of view, when we hear others slandering us, it's normal to retaliate with the principle "if others leave me alone, I'll leave them alone; if they attack me, I'll certainly fight back." However, from the Mahayana Buddhist point of view, this is an attitude we should give up. What we need to do is to take defeat upon ourselves and give victory to others.

When first hearing this, some people may think, "If I take loss and defeat upon myself no matter what happens, how can I survive?"

Such worries are unnecessary. Authentic practice progresses stage by stage. For ordinary people, do what you are able; you don't have to take loss on everything immediately.

However, during your daily associations with others, you should learn various skills to prevent the arising of afflictive emotions. For example, when you're cursed by others, treat what you hear as echoes in a valley, which can't do harm or benefit to you.

In the old days, once Hanshan asked Shide, "If I am slandered, bullied, insulted, mocked, belittled, humiliated, loathed, or deceived by a worldly person, what should I do? Shide replied, "Just bear him, tolerate him, allow him, avoid him, endure him, respect him, or leave him alone, and then look at him after a couple of years."[16]

This isn't only a pith instruction of mind training, but also a beautiful prescription for conducting oneself among others. Suppose you hadn't done anything wrong to others, but they insisted on framing you. What do you think would work better, striking back or applying this approach? Smart people would choose the latter.

However, secrets are only in the hands of very few wise men; they're not known by the majority. And even when coming across these secrets occasionally, very few people could apply them in reality.

Buddhadharma has to be practiced. The statement "May I take loss and defeat upon myself and give the gain and victory to others" is difficult to apply in the beginning, but if you persevere for a long time, it will go easily. If you could practice it with a single-pointed mind, just one sentence could uproot all your suffering.

The sixth secret to happiness: those who requite my kindness with enmity are my guru.

Root text:

> Even if someone whom I have helped
> and placed great hope upon
> frames me irrationally,
> may I view him as my spiritual teacher.

Commentarial note: Suppose I've helped and placed great hope upon someone, but later on, instead of repaying my kindness, this person frames me. Even in this scenario, may I view him or her as my spiritual teacher.

Nowadays, lots of people requite others' kindness with enmity. Some enterprisers take trouble to provide training for an employee, but after becoming capable, instead of making contributions to this company, the employee seduces customers to his own startup, leaving his boss at a loss.

In the eyes of worldly people, such a person is very hateful. But according to Mahayana Buddhism, not only should we give up bearing grudges, but we should also treat those who harm us as gurus.

To many people, this is unimaginable. But in the history of Buddhism, many great masters have manifested such a stance in their actual conduct.

Once, a disciple of the elder monk Guang Qin was framed by others and went to see his teacher. After the disciple cried over his grievances, Guang Qin said, "Vulgar! So worldly! Only mundane people think others are provoking oneself. A practitioner's mind should be set on the path. When mistreated by others, one thinks they're urging oneself to improve their practice."

Therefore, as a practitioner, when others frame you, it's the greatest kindness.

Even if we can't actualize this stance, we should at least think about others' kindness and forget their disservice. However, many people react in the opposite way: right after they're helped by others, they completely forget it as though nothing had happened. Meanwhile, an unpleasant remark uttered many years ago is remembered vividly and clearly. This isn't good. We should get rid of this habit and stop harboring grudges in our hearts. Too many grievances will hurt oneself and others.

The seventh secret to happiness: all the good deeds you've done in this life will be rewarded.

Root text:

May I directly and indirectly
offer help and happiness to all my mothers
and secretly take upon myself
all sorts of sufferings from them.

Commentarial note: With direct or indirect approaches, may I offer all kinds of happiness to sentient beings, and secretly take their sufferings upon myself.

Benefiting others can be direct or indirect. Direct examples are doctors curing the diseases of patients, teachers dispelling the confusion of students, and so forth. Indirect examples could be helping sentient beings become free from their suffering, such as helping animals by not eating meat.

Benefiting sentient beings appears to help others, but in fact, it helps oneself.

I heard a story about an American man named Klaus. One night, he was trapped in the wilderness after his car broke down in a snowstorm. He was anxious and desperate, but a man on horseback appeared in front of him. After figuring out what was going on, without hesitation, the man towed Klaus's car to the nearest town with his horse.

When Klaus offered money out of gratitude for the man's assistance, he refused, saying, "I don't need any reward, but please promise one thing for me. When you see anyone in difficulty, please try your best to help them too."

Afterward, Klaus helped countless people, and in each case he asked whomever he had helped to make the same promise.

Many years later, Klaus was trapped again, but this time on an isolated island after a flash flood. However, he was saved by a young boy at the risk of his life. He thanked the young man gratefully, and in their conversation, realized that he had once helped this boy as well, which was reaffirmed when the boy asked him to make the same promise that he asked countless people to make: "I don't need any reward, but please promise one thing for me. When you see anyone in difficulty, please try your best to help them too."

Klaus suddenly realized that all the good deeds he had done were actually done for himself.

Benefiting others is benefiting oneself. This has been explained comprehensively and thoroughly in Mahayana Buddhism. For instance, *The Guide to the Bodhisattva's Way of Life* tells us:

> Whatever joy there is in this world
> comes from desiring others to be happy,
> and whatever suffering there is in this world
> comes from desiring oneself to be happy. (Chapter 8, Verse
> 129)

You may feel strange if this is your first time coming across altruistic instructions in Mahayana Buddhism. However, if you examine these teachings carefully, you'll find this idea to be valuable.

The eighth secret to happiness: all phenomena are like dreams and illusions.

Root text:

> May all my practices
> not be stained by thoughts of the eight worldly concerns;
> with the wisdom of knowing all phenomena are like illusions,
> may I attain liberation free from attachment and bondage.

Commentarial note: May all my conduct be unstained by the eight worldly concerns. May I recognize that all phenomena have an empty essence yet dreamlike appearance. May I be free from attachment and bondage and attain liberation.

The eight worldly concerns are praise and blame, disrepute and fame, gain and loss, suffering and happiness.

As ordinary people, we like to be praised and dislike being blamed. We want others' attention and don't want to be neglected. We wish to gain what we want and don't like to lose it. We want to be happy and dislike suffering.

However, since practitioners have the recognition that all phenomena are empty by nature—"all conditioned phenomena are like dreams, illusions, water bubbles and reflections"—they don't place great importance on loss and gain, so they're able to free themselves from the bondage of the eight worldly concerns.

Only when we rid ourselves of all of these attachments can we truly be free from suffering.

Whoever has an altruistic mind will have happiness.

These eight secrets have explained the principles of benefiting others in different aspects. Whether you follow Buddhism or not, as long as you practice accordingly, you'll attain happiness.

Altruism isn't just the root of Mahayana Buddhism, but also the indispensable fortune of mankind. This is the twenty-first century, but even when we reach the thirtieth century, we human beings will still need it; it will never become outdated.

All of our unhappy experiences stem from attachment to "I." Only by transforming our mind using this transitory life to benefit others can we decrease suffering and increase happiness.

This isn't exceptional to Buddhism. It's also true for other religions. Mother Teresa spent her entire life helping others and lived an extremely simple life. However, she didn't suffer as a result of her efforts—her life was full of joy and happiness.

Many people don't know this secret but only complain about their misfortune and the unfairness of the gods. If you don't want to be happy, then that's another story, but if you do wish to be happy, please stop complaining to others about your circumstances and start cultivating an altruistic mind from now on.

My practice isn't good, but I've read a great number of sutras and commentaries. From my reading, I strongly feel that what we human beings need most is the altruistic mind. Whoever has it will attain happiness.

The profundity and subtlety of this can only be comprehended when you truly embrace it and achieve it.

Of course, there are gaps between the altruistic minds of ordinary people and bodhisattvas. Even if we can't reach a high state, we should at least make progress on the path of decreasing selfishness and increasing altruism. Even one step forward is a good start.

Q&A

I've visited many temples in Chinese areas and was deceived into buying expensive joss sticks in almost all of them. So, my question is whether similar scenarios also occur in Tibetan Buddhist temples? How does Buddhism treat this?

Nowadays, commercialization in temples in Chinese areas has become more and more severe. In some places, temples are even treated as publicly traded companies and have drawn great attention from the public. If this scenario continues to escalate, Buddhism may face a crisis.

However, I was told that the United Front Work Department and the National Development and Reform Commission have issued documentation to stop temples from being publicly traded or contracted. If these policies could be implemented, it would benefit Buddhism.

So far, I haven't seen this happening in Tibetan areas. Except for a couple of famous monasteries, most monasteries follow the old tradition.

Personally, I'm against the idea of selling admission tickets to monasteries, because it will cause people to mistake monasteries for tourist sites. As Buddhist facilities, they should be pure and tranquil, and provide visitors a sense of peace and auspiciousness.

What are the differences between mundane happiness and supramundane happiness? How do I achieve supramundane happiness?
Mundane happiness originates from sensory enjoyment, while supramundane happiness transcends sensory enjoyment.

In order to achieve supramundane happiness, we should first cultivate the mind of renunciation and understand that cyclic existence is full of suffering. Afterward, we need to generate the bodhichitta of placing all sentient beings in buddhahood. Finally, we should realize that all phenomena are empty. In this way, we can attain indescribable happiness and peace.

Countless great masters throughout history have already realized such a state. So, as long as we have enough devotion and diligence, I believe everyone can achieve this.

Some people take ordination after experiences of living as house-holders in this society, while some become monks or nuns when they're still young. Are there any differences in terms of their enlightenment?

In regard to enlightenment, it doesn't matter whether you take ordination as a child or later in life. The key is whether you have enough devotion and diligence. If your devotion and diligence aren't adequate, then even if you become a monk or nun in childhood, you may not be able to become enlightened. However, if you have devotion and diligence to the fullest extent, then even if you take ordination very late in life, you may become enlightened very soon.

You mentioned earlier that causes in past lives result in effects in the present life. In this way, if I do good deeds, can it change my fate in the present? Or do I have to wait for future lives?

It depends on how you practice virtue. In Buddhadharma, it says that if you practice immense virtue with objects such as buddhas, noble beings, or the noble sangha, the effect could fully ripen in this very life.

The law of karmic cause and effect is complex. Only after systematic study can you understand its profundity and sub-tlety. To put it simply, any karma you accumulate in this life could have three categories of effects. Firstly, it could fully ripen in this life, which is called the effect fully ripened in the present life. Secondly, it could fully ripen in the next life. Third, it could ripen anytime from the next till hundreds and thousands of lifetimes from now.

Just like criminals, some are sent to prisons immediately, some are sentenced to jail after a couple of years, and some may never be punished in this life.

Since all phenomena are empty by nature, why should we pursue happiness?

It's true that all phenomena are empty by nature, and once you reach this level of realization, there's no need to pursue happiness because you've already attained the ultimate state of happiness, just like a person who gets a PhD must have mastered the basics in elementary school. However, before you reach that level of realization, you must wish to be happy.

The empty nature of all phenomena is described in terms of the nature of ultimate reality, while the pursuit of happiness is described at the phenomenal level. We should avoid confusing these two.

For instance, scientifically speaking, in the eyes of physicists, a cup is made up of small particles like atoms, but in their daily life, they wouldn't deny the existence of the cup and its function of holding water. Similarly, people who study the Dharma shouldn't deny the phenomenal existence of an object due to its empty nature at the ultimate level of reality.

Chan Master Yongjia Xuanjue (665–713) said, "The six realms vividly appear in one's dream, yet the three-thousand-fold universe is completely empty after waking up." The suffering and happiness of sentient beings in the six realms are like in dreams, but before we wake up from the dream of samsara, all the sensations exist without failure. Only when we perfectly realize the emptiness of all phenomena can we stop pursuing happiness and shunning suffering.

Which creates more happiness: loving someone or being loved by someone?

It's up to you. Happiness is a sensation in the heart. Being loved by someone or loving someone—whichever makes you feel satisfied can create more happiness for you.

One of my friends lost his job after suffering from depression. Another friend constantly wants to commit suicide. Is this caused by negative karma in previous lives? What should my friends do?
No matter what we experience, we should never choose suicide. We should face life with courage instead. Life matters for everyone. As long as the tree-covered mountain exists, there's no need to worry about firewood: similarly, it doesn't matter if we have no money or job temporarily—everything will be all right as time goes on.

The causes of mental illness are quite complicated. If it stems from previous karma, then it's hard to counteract. However, if it's the result of nonhuman interference, reciting the mantra of Padmasambhava—*om ah hum vajra guru padma siddhi hum*—often can improve things gradually.

According to Tibetan medicine, the majority of diseases are caused by nonhumans. When haunted by them, whether you believe in Buddhism or not, reciting the mantra of Padmasambhava can always help you to get rid of such states.

Besides, if you run into trouble in daily life, reciting this mantra can help too. I do this a lot. Sometimes I'll have a bad dream, and when I wake up, I immediately recite this mantra one hundred times and my mind calms down right away.

It's easy to restrain body and speech, for instance, avoiding killing and adopting a vegetarian diet. However, it's hard to control our mind. How should we prevent impure thoughts then?
Compared to body and speech, it's more difficult to control our mind. This is why the Buddha taught in the order

of body, speech, and mind. So, first adjust our body, then speech, and finally mind.

In order to tame our mind, a process is required. If you train and tame your mind according to the instructions of the Buddha, it will gradually become pliant and finally reach the purest state.

Helping others makes me happy. However, since my abilities are limited, sometimes I feel helpless to help others, which makes me feel quite sad. If my abilities are insignificant, does it mean what I'm doing is meaningless? Should I keep helping others?

When doing virtuous deeds, one can encounter many obstacles, but when committing misdeeds, things often go smoothly. But even if this is the case, we shouldn't withdraw our intention to help others. However much we're able to do, we should just do it.

Here's a story. One day after the tide ebbed, a shoal of small fish was trapped in a shallow rock pit on the beach. Their small pool was becoming heated by the hot air, and they were struggling desperately. Seeing this, a child picked up the fish and threw them into the ocean one after another. An adult mocked, "Do you know what you're doing? How can you spare them all? Who cares?" Without slowing down, the child kept picking up the fish and replied, "This little fish cares." "This fish cares." "This fish cares too." Similarly, while helping others, we may not be able to make a great difference, and we often encounter obstacles. However, we should never lose heart, because there's always someone who cares.

I know a master who has a monastery of over five hundred residents. On one occasion, his approach to spreading the Dharma and benefiting sentient beings wasn't accepted by some people, which made him quite vexed. One night, he came to see me and told me that he didn't want to be an abbot anymore and was prepared to give up everything. I advised him, "Just keep doing. If it's for oneself, it might be painful, but if it's for the benefit of sentient beings without selfish thoughts, even if you don't succeed, it won't be too bad." Finally, he took my advice and continued his course.

In the process of benefiting others, don't give up easily. As long as we can breathe, we should spare no efforts to help sentient beings.

How can lay practitioners remain diligent all the time?
There are indeed a great deal of causes and conditions that can distract us from Dharma study. However, as a person who has taken refuge in the Three Jewels, we should plan well our everyday life. Get up early in the morning and go to sleep late at night, limit your contact with distracting circumstances, and make time to study and practice the Dharma.

I've been studying Tibetan Buddhism and I do guru yoga every day. My question is whether guru yoga is a form of meditation?
Meditation falls into two categories: analytic meditation and calm-abiding meditation.

When practicing guru yoga, we visualize our guru in front of us, think of him as the embodiment of all the buddhas of the three times, and pray to him devotedly—this is analytic meditation. Afterward, we visualize our guru radiating light rays, which dissolve into our body so that the wisdom of our guru and our own mind become one. We abide in this state. This is calm-abiding meditation.

Therefore, guru yoga is meditation.

Which creates more merit: spending two hours performing pros-
trations and chanting prayers but neither listening to Dharma
teachings nor reading Dharma texts, or the other way around?
Which gives you more nutrition: eating rice without an
entrée or the other way around?

The six realms of cyclic existence are like a gigantic machine.
Sentient beings are like parts of the machine, while the compas-
sionate Buddha, standing beside this machine, keeps rescuing
suffering beings from it. I want to ask, Who made this machine?
What keeps it running?
Cyclic existence is unlimited, so it's not appropriate to compare it to a limited machine.

Nobody drives cyclic existence. It's a natural law that sentient beings migrate in it. Just like a poisoned seed yielding
poisonous fruit, after committing negative actions, sentient
beings are bound to be born in cyclic existence. Without
stopping the accumulation of karma, there's no end. This
isn't controlled by someone externally.

If you want to know more about cyclic existence, you
need to study the four noble truths and the twelve linking
factors of dependent origination in Buddhism. After you
understand these principles, you'll figure out how cyclic
existence works.

If the mind of the past is unfindable, the mind of the present is
unfindable, and the mind of the future is unfindable, is a mind
pursing happiness findable?
If we're talking about the nature of ultimate realty, the minds
of the three times are unfindable, as is the mind pursing happiness. Upon reaching this state, we would be as unfettered

and at ease as Jetsun Milarepa in Tibet and the monk Ji Gong in China.[17]

However, before reaching such a state of realization, our mind still recognizes happiness and fears suffering, so pursuing happiness doesn't give rise to any problems.

Pursuing happiness falls into two categories: the temporary happiness of inner contentment, and the ultimate happiness of removing cognitive obscurations and the obscurations of mental afflictions, as well as attaining the fruition of noble beings.

I've read something like this: "There are three levels of realization in one's life. The first level is 'you see mountains as mountains, and rivers as rivers'; the second level is 'you see mountains not as mountains, and rivers not as rivers'; the third level is 'you see mountains still as mountains, and rivers still as rivers." Would you please explain what this means?

Before you study any Dharma, you have the strong belief that all phenomena exist intrinsically. Therefore, you see mountains as mountains and rivers as rivers. After studying the Dharma, through analysis of the theories of the Middle Way, you understand that all phenomena are empty by nature, so you see mountains not as mountains and rivers not as rivers. After you've attained some realization through Dharma study, you understand that nothing is findable, but at the same time, we need to comply with sentient beings at the level of appearances, so you see mountains still as mountains and rivers still as rivers.

Take happiness for example. It can also reflect these three levels of comprehension. Firstly, before you engage in Dharma study, you think happiness is real; secondly, after Dharma study, you realize that happiness is empty by nature; and finally, although you have some inconceivable realization, you admit the existence of happiness in order to comply with sentient beings.

It's worth mentioning that it's essential to comply with sentient beings! Although the Buddha had attained the highest level of realization, when in the presence of others, he acted as an ordinary person, begging for food with his bowl and eating meals. Many great practitioners also have acted in this way. They have enviable inner realization, but the same external appearance as ordinary people.

What is Theravada Buddhism? What is Mahayana Buddhism? Which one should we choose?

Theravada Buddhism (the Basic Vehicle) is often called Southern Buddhism, because it's very popular in Sri Lanka, Burma, and so forth. Mahayana Buddhism (the Great Vehicle) includes Chinese Buddhism and Tibetan Buddhism.

Venerable Atisha said, "The distinction between the Basic Vehicle and the Great Vehicle depends on the presence or absence of bodhichitta." With bodhichitta, it's the Great Vehicle; without bodhichitta, it's the Basic Vehicle.

If you only wish to attain happiness and be free from suffering for yourself, it's an aspiration of the Basic Vehicle. Besides individual liberation, if you wish to liberate all sentient beings, it's an aspiration of the Great Vehicle.

Some people wish to be reborn in the Pure Land through reciting buddhas' names, but if you ask them why they want to go there, they say that it's in order to enjoy life in the Pure Land of Great Bliss. In this way, although their practice belongs to the Great Vehicle, their aspiration belongs to the Basic Vehicle.

Choosing the Great Vehicle or Basic Vehicle depends on your own inclinations. If you have a strong wish to liberate sentient beings regardless of your own liberation, then you can choose the Great Vehicle.

When practicing guru yoga, should I visualize my root guru as Padmasambhava?
There are two ways. In *Finding Comfort and Ease in the Illusoriness of Things*, Longchenpa states, "When practicing guru yoga, there is no need to change the appearance of the guru. Just visualize the way your guru is." However, there are also other instructions suggesting that you should visualize the guru as Padmasambhava with the essence of your root guru.

Whether you should visualize the image of your guru or Padmasambhava depends on your faith. If your faith in your guru is the same as your faith in the Buddha, then you can visualize his image. If not, then, it's better to visualize Padmasambhava as your guru.

If all phenomena are like a dream, why is a misdeed in a dream not counted as a misdeed, while a misdeed while awake is counted?
According to the view of individual liberation, a transgression in a dream does involve some kind of fault, but since there's no actual object for this misdeed, it isn't counted as a real violation.

Chandrakirti describes three kinds of dreams: the first are the dreams we experience in sleep, the second are the dreams of life that we're experiencing right now, and the third are the dreams that constitutes everything happening before we reach enlightenment.

We haven't yet awakened from the dream of samsara. Once we attain enlightenment, we'll realize every misdeed we've done is like a misdeed in a dream that can't do any harm to us.

My life is quite unpleasant so far. Is there anything I can do to transform my life?

The only way to transform our life is to do virtuous deeds. Buddhism believes that the course of one's life is determined by this person's karma, but it's not inalterable. If you engage in a great number of virtuous deeds, your life will turn in a better direction. If you've read the *Four Lessons of Liao Fan*, you'll fully understand this.

Once we realize that suffering is the hue of life, our sense of suffering will become less obvious. For instance, when sick, although the physical discomfort is unbearable, the mental suffering caused by an unhealthy mindset could be completely eliminated.

As a matter of fact, you must have a very happy life. If you get a chance to visit a prison, you'll understand the kind of life that's truly unpleasant. I've visited some prisons. For many prisoners, their only wish is to have a one-hour conversation with their loved ones. Meanwhile, you can chat with your friends and loved ones at any time, every day. However, many of us don't cherish this opportunity and argue and quarrel with those who are close to us. If you were in prison, you'd feel extremely content to chat with them just once.

So, reflect on this and give up the idea that you're suffering badly. If you always complain in this way, you'll add extra unhappiness to your life. We should follow the course our conditions take us when dealing with good or bad and success or failure. Of course, this doesn't mean being passive. For any meaningful activity, we should never give up easily and instead spare no effort when working on it.

I've been a vegetarian for a long time, but I've been forced to take lives sometimes. For instance, when friends treat me to a meal, they ask the restaurant to kill an animal specifically for us. What should I do?

In general, Buddhists wouldn't ask for anything to be killed. However, at a wedding or New Year's Eve festival, tons of creatures are killed, and some Buddhists have to treat it with courtesy, so they're defiled with misdeeds. If this is the case, engage in purification practices as much as you can.

In my life, killing is the thing I'm most unwilling to witness. When I was little, whenever I saw yaks about to be slaughtered, I would make every effort to stop it. If I couldn't prevent this from happening, I would run far away because I didn't have the heart to see the cruelty.

Based on the law of karmic cause and effect, the consequence of killing is extremely horrific. If someone kills frequently, apart from this person's own misfortune, even his or her offspring will suffer as a result of their negative actions. Therefore, I hope you'll do your best to give up taking lives of any kind.

Can vegetarians eat eggs and drink milk?

In order to be vegan, eggs and milk shouldn't be taken. However, generally speaking, if the eggs aren't fertilized, they don't have the potential to become real lives, so some vegetarians also eat eggs.

Cyclic existence is full of suffering. In this world, no food, including rice and vegetables, is free from negative karma because during the process of growing crops killing insects is inevitable. So, any food involves misdeeds of some kind.

In general, eating eggs and drinking milk cause suffering to animals indirectly, but the consequence isn't as severe as that of consuming meat, so it's relatively easier to purify.

My mother suffers from cancer. How can I help her?
People often question the effects of negative karma until they get an incurable disease, but by then it's too late. We should examine our actions—which are negative and which are positive—and adopt positive actions and abandon negative ones. Only in this way can we avoid regrets in the future. This is the heartfelt advice of a monk from the Qinghai-Tibet Plateau.

In my conversations with professors here, someone mentioned that by reciting the names of buddhas, some patients with cancer are miraculously cured. Therefore, if you have cancer, if you can engage in virtuous deeds like reciting the mantra of Avalokiteshvara and the names of buddhas as well as releasing captured animals, it will be helpful.

I hope you can advise your mother to recite the names of buddhas. Regardless of whether it will save her life or not, it will still benefit her greatly.

The Buddha advocates renouncing secular life, while Confucius promotes engaging in mundane life. The Buddha values spiritual wealth, while Confucius seeks realistic goals. What's your opinion of Confucius?
Buddhism doesn't just emphasize renunciation but also teaches how to wisely engage in secular life. In today's talk,

I integrated both aspects. If I had only talked about supramundane theories like emptiness and bodhichitta, you may not have accepted it.

Confucianism doesn't neglect spiritual wealth either. However, in comparison with Buddhism, there's greater emphasis on how to take care of the present life. Confucianism talks more about how to conduct oneself and how to be dutiful to parents, but it doesn't offer a thorough analysis of how to teach and free sentient beings in future lives.

In fact, Confucianism and Buddhism are the indispensable essence of traditional culture in China. Mr. Nan Huaijin once said, "Only when Confucianism, Buddhism, and Daoism are integrated can Chinese people achieve comprehensive enhancement. If one of them is missing, it won't be perfect."

Personally, I'm very interested in traditional culture. When reading books, I like to read books by ancient authors. I hope you can learn more about traditional culture and assimilate the wisdom of ancient teachers.

Lecture at Shanghai Jiao Tong University
October 24, 2012

12. HEART

Doubt isn't something to fear. The key is how to deal with it.

Q&A

If I've helped a person and he harms others in the future, am I also at fault?
If you don't have an intent to harm others, you won't be at fault.

I financially supported a poor student and wished him a promising future, but to my disappointment, he harmed many people with the knowledge he acquired. Was I wrong to help him? No, because my intention was to benefit him. The wrongdoing he committed will only bring negative results on himself, not me.

So he himself will be responsible for this karma?
Correct. I helped him with a good heart, and a good heart will never bear negative results. Karma depends on intention and action. If my intention and actions are pure and I don't facilitate any negative deeds, then he has to suffer the consequences of whatever wrongdoing he commits.

In other words, it's judged by intention.
Right. Virtue and nonvirtue depend on intention.

Some people aren't very good looking, but you just want to be close to them. Is this because of their charm or something else?
It might be due to certain causes and conditions.

In Buddhism, we believe that hidden causes and conditions may cause you to feel someone is special at first sight: "Hmm, did I meet him before?" "Why do I feel so close to him?"

There are two possible explanations for this. If this person is a great master, a qualified spiritual teacher, the joyful feeling and pure perception caused by him will bring you liberation and happiness.

If this person is an ordinary worldly person, your attachment to him might come from your collective aspiration in previous lives: "May we be together life after life." It also might be an opposite scenario: he was your enemy in previous lives, and because of the debts between you, there's a sense of "you owe me" and "I owe you."

It's hard to say whether you were close or hostile to each other. Causes and conditions are complicated—sometimes they involve many lifetimes.

Recently I've been translating the biography of Mingyur Dorjé (1645–1667). As the revealer of the Namchö (Sky Dharma) of the Palyul lineage of the Nyingma school, he was able to recall things from over two hundred lifetimes. Sometimes he became an animal, sometimes he became a human being—there were various situations. From those stories, we can see that he had a close relationship with his guru Chagme Rinpoché (1613–1678) over the course of many lifetimes. For instance, on one occasion, his guru was born as a horse and he too was born as a small horse. There are many stories like this.

Anyway, after reading such things, you feel the power of karma. When you reflect on people you've met in this life, either your guru or other people, you'll realize that there must be causes and conditions reaching back many lifetimes.

In the Chinese area, disciples have great difficulty choosing a lama. If the lama holds strict discipline and appears conservative, disciples are afraid to approach him. If he's talented and erudite, he's often at the same time too unrestrained. So how should we make an appropriate choice?

No matter whether he or she is conservative or liberal, it's critical that one examine the lama first.

Relying on a lama on impulse always results in unpleasant stories: the faith of the disciple wavers, the blessing of the lama vanishes, or the disciple slanders the lama and the lama lambastes the disciple. This is because prior examination is missing.

Relying on a lama after examining him would less likely lead a disciple to withdraw. If the lama is qualified, no matter what he emanates, the disciple is supposed to continue relying on him with faith and follow the examples of relying on a qualified teacher outlined in the *Avatamsaka Sutra*.

Lamas who hold pure precepts may be conservative, and many lamas are like this in the monasteries of Tibet. They don't have many opportunities to visit Chinese areas, and even when they do, due to language barriers and their serious demeanor, people find they aren't easy to approach. However, if you could study under such a lama, they would prod and supervise you from time to time, which is very beneficial for your practice.

Liberal lamas are relatively easygoing. If they have skillful means and are also versed in Buddhadharma, when you rely on them, you can learn the Dharma in a lighthearted atmosphere. This is very good too.

In general, external character isn't the key. The key is whether you can learn Buddhadharma from him.

It's a pity that many people don't understand this. When relying on a lama, they rely on their smile and behavior with some affectionate attachment. However, this affection could change. After relying on a lama for a while, if you find you haven't learned any Dharma at all, once your affection changes, your faith will decrease as well. You won't be able to rely on this lama any longer. Even if this isn't the case, once impermanence shows up, the lama disappears forever. Without having received the Dharma, you'll be miserable.

Therefore, it's critical to make connections through the Dharma. This is the genuine meaning of relying on a lama.

When setting animals free, if they're fish, some of them die and some are fished by other people. If they're birds, some of them don't fly and then people toss them up in the air. Is this kind of treatment of animals negative? Is this accumulating merit or committing negative karma?

It's been more than twenty years since I made the aspiration to set animals free and started asking others to do it. I like this virtuous deed in particular.

What you've mentioned does happen. Some people are against freeing animals and think it has disadvantages.

However, we shouldn't say that setting animals free is meaningless. I believe that setting animals free is a 100 percent virtuous practice with immense merit. However, we do need to pay attention to our approach. Otherwise, we aren't acting responsibly with their precious lives.

Before we release any creatures, we need to ask: Is this the right location? Will they survive here? Some people released birds on a highway. After setting them free, some birds couldn't fly right away and were crushed to death by oncoming vehicles.

Experienced people find a good location for the animals to be released. Sometimes it takes them several days. This is a safe way to do it.

I'm in a group dedicated to releasing animals, and members are encouraged to make the aspiration to have a vegetarian diet for their entire life. However, as it's said, "The Buddhadharma cannot be realized in isolation from worldly life." Occasionally, I have to eat meat. So, how should I deal with conflicts like this?
It's best to adopt a vegetarian diet for your entire life. However, if you can't avoid eating meat sometimes, avoid it while you participate in the activities of releasing animals. Otherwise, if you release animals while you consume their flesh, the virtuous deed is defiled.

"The Buddhadharma cannot be realized in isolation from worldly life" reminds us to conform with secular life while practicing the Dharma and learning to realize the truth of worldly existence. It doesn't mean that since worldly people eat meat, I have to eat it; or since worldly people steal, I should also become a thief; or since worldly people commit criminal acts, I should follow their example. This certainly isn't the case. There are things that we should comply with, and some that we should never comply with.

Your books have been available for sale. I'm reading them and also recommend them to my friends. Can we perfect our practice through reading books like these?
Tales for Transforming Adversity and Achieve by Doing feature theories and stories I've taught during lectures. They're in plain language to make them easy for worldly people to understand. Each chapter isn't long, so you can finish them very quickly.

Through reading these books, you may encounter some new ideas, realize that what you've done before may not have been appropriate, and learn how to conduct yourself, how to become kind, and how to accumulate merit in the future. They also touch on the subject of death.

In regard to whether they could help someone perfect his or her practice, this depends on different individual's faculties. If someone has superior faculties, listening to a simple instruction could lead them to recognize the nature of mind. In such cases, enlightenment shouldn't be excluded.

My management job causes me too much stress. When focusing on Dharma study, I don't have much interest in my job; yet when focusing on my job, I find the Dharma is alien to me. How can I find the balance between working and practicing?
This is a very important question for many people. If you gave up your practice, you'd regret wasting this human life that's so hard to obtain, so you have to practice. But when you do practice, your job can make you too busy to maintain it. I often suggest that people live their life in practice and practice in their daily life.

In fact, this isn't that difficult. For us Tibetan people, practice has been well integrated into daily life and has become habitual since childhood. Once the habit is formed, practice comes naturally.

If you take practice and work to be incompatible, not working while practicing and not practicing while working, you may never have time to practice. As lay practitioners, everybody has family and a job to take care of. It's unrealistic to give them all up. It's even hard just to go on retreat for a week or a month.

Therefore, you need to get used to practicing while working. For instance, read three or four pages of the *Words of My Perfect Teacher* every day, or recite a certain number of mantras while commuting by car or walking. Once the habit is formed, your practice won't be interrupted.

Some people go too far. They give up their job when practicing and have to go back to work when their family and life put them under unbearable stress. But once they start working again, they give up their practice altogether.

I don't agree with this approach. If you can't choose between living a normal life as an ordinary person and taking ordination as a monastic, you'd better give consideration to both—live in practice and practice in daily life. In fact, during the time of Buddha Shakyamuni, the majority of disciples were householders who took care of both living and practicing. If this was the case then, why shouldn't it be the same in modern times?

So, on one hand, take good care of your job and family. On the other hand, make some time to study the Dharma every day.

There's no doubt that we can make time for practice one or two hours every day. I'm acquainted with some entrepreneurs who are extremely busy and have to travel around the world. However, when they find time in their day, they spend every minute on Dharma study and daily chanting. They've taken good care of both worldly obligations and Buddhist practice for a long time, and there's no sign that they'll withdraw from their practice.

This is also true for myself. Every day I have to spend time on translation, giving teachings, management of our institute, taking care of a couple of construction projects, and remotely managing schools. Sometimes, I also need to travel to cities to exchange ideas with you. However, I've never skipped my daily prayers. When I'm on tour, I finish part of my daily chanting on airplanes or in cars. When I get some time to be alone, I do a little bit of translation. Sometimes it may be just a couple of stanzas, but it's acceptable, and I've persevered in this way for all these years.

In order to persevere, you have to abstain from impulse. You should avoid sometimes practicing with single-pointed focus and enormous enthusiasm, caring about nothing else, while at other times feeling hopeless and giving up your practice. If you follow this pattern, you won't be able to do your job or practice well. We should be consistent and never give up our commitment.

You don't have to give up work, because you need to survive. You also shouldn't give up practice, because this will fulfill your wish for liberation. As long as you don't give up, there's always a way to balance life and practice so that they can move forward simultaneously.

Since I started Dharma study, I've quit drinking alcohol, eating
meat, and singing karaoke. However, at parties, I'm marginal-
ized and people think I'm weird. What should I do in these situ-
ations?

When quitting drinking and meat eating can cause a Buddhist's secular social circle to shrink, there are two ways to
deal with this.

Firstly, let it go. If your change of lifestyle decreases the
number of unwholesome friends you have, it's good that your
life has become simpler. These days people say, "No liquor,
no party." They think that if you refuse to drink, you're not
their buddy. If you don't indulge in entertainment, you must
be a nut who's brainwashed by some bizarre ideas. What's
wrong with Dharma study? It's just people's preconceptions
about it.

Secondly, you can explain to your friends that you've
stopped drinking because of health reasons. For instance,
"My doctor said that if I don't quit drinking, I'll die." "If I
keep eating meat, my blood pressure will never go down."
Gradually, people will just accept it.

In fact, vegetarian food is fashionable now. Some Tibetan
folks advised me, "You can't quit eating meat. You'll suffer
from malnutrition." I said, "You know, Barack Obama recommends a vegetarian diet." I read that he recommends
being vegetarian for environmental protection and his wife
and daughters have also propagated the vegetarian diet in
some universities.

However, in some social circles, drinking, eating meat,
and karaoke are still important, though this is gradually
changing. You may try to change their minds about this, and
if you fail, make sure to protect yourself with skillful means.

I have meditation sessions at night, so I have to leave right after my job's regular office hours. My boss came to talk with me after he found out that I don't work overtime. How can I avoid displeasing my boss while at the same time continuing my meditation?

This also requires skillful means. In this case, you need to examine, reflect, and pray repeatedly. I believe that combining the wisdom of the bodhisattva Manjushri, the great compassion of the bodhisattva Avalokiteshvara, and your own skillful means will produce a great solution.

Can I lie to my boss for the sake of meditation? Does this fall into the category of wrong speech—telling lies?

It could be called lying for a virtuous purpose. What do you plan to say?

A master told me that reciting mantras while doing something else doesn't create any merit; only reciting mantras with a peaceful mind during a meditation session can do this. I made the aspiration to recite a mantra one hundred thousand times. After he said this, my heart sank. What's your opinion on this?

From my point of view, it's okay to recite mantras while you're doing something else, such as walking and the like. You may not be as focused as when you're reciting mantras with a peaceful mind in meditation, but for experienced practitioners, there's no big difference.

In Tibet, many great masters are able to recite mantras while walking, sitting, or lying down. They've gotten used to it. In the past, there was a geshé who could read books on Buddhist logic and the *Abhidharmakosha* and recite mantras simultaneously. He could completely comprehend the contents of the book and finish a great number of mantras with satisfied effect. My teacher, Jigme Phuntsok Rinpoche, could also recite mantras in his dreams while sleeping. On a few occasions, I witnessed that he had fallen asleep already, but his fingers were still rolling the mala.

We haven't yet reached this state. However, reciting mantras while working on something else absolutely generates merit. The master who said you have to recite mantras while meditating might be talking about it from a strict point of view, but it's true that when you recite during a meditation session, your mind is more peaceful, which results in greater merit.

What's your daily life like? When do you get up in the morning? What do you do every day? Do you mind telling us, so that we can follow you as an example?

Take today as an example. I got up at 5:30 in the morning, recited mantras for half an hour, meditated for a while, and chanted my daily prayers for an hour. Afterward, I made one hundred prostrations. Then, I drank Manjushri tea from Mount Wutai while reading books. Then, I wrote my microblog post for today. After having breakfast, I came here.

When do you usually go to bed then?

According to some old study, it's said that human beings need to sleep at least eight hours per night, but in some newly reported research that was published this year, it says that people who sleep over eight hours will die sooner, and that four to five hours are long enough for us. Therefore, oversleeping is bad for your health.

Usually, I go to bed after 12 o'clock. Last night, I went to bed a bit late because a sick person in my hometown asked me to wait to chant prayers for him. However, he didn't call me until 1 AM, so I went to sleep after that.

When do you write or translate?
Usually in the afternoon.

In Samantabhadra's Aspiration to Good Actions, *it's said that we should "serve sentient beings so as to suit their needs." But I've found this is too difficult. Sentient beings can be virtuous and vicious, right and wrong. We can try to meet the needs of virtuous sentient beings, but what should we do for vicious ones with wicked needs? Should we comply with them?*
"Serve sentient beings so as to suit their needs" refers to complying with them all the time. This is a supreme skillful means for benefiting sentient beings taught to bodhisattvas in Mahayana sutras such as the *Avatamsaka Sutra*.

In the *Song of Victory*, Jigme Phuntsok Rinpoché also states, "Let your speech and behavior always serve friends so as to suit their needs." Some people once raised a question, "If we conform to everyone, should we let desire arise for greedy people and hatred arise for angry people?"

Jigme Phuntsok Rinpoche said, "To meet the needs of sentient beings, bodhisattvas must have the wisdom and capability to liberate them. For instance, in order to liberate the concubines of the king, the bodhisattva Manjushri complied with them first, and then asked them to take refuge, and finally led them to liberation."

Many bodhisattvas, not only the bodhisattva Manjushri, comply with worldly people to liberate them in various circumstances with their skillful means.

Therefore, if you have the ability and skillful means, when

facing "vicious sentient beings," you might listen to them first to gain their trust. For example, if you'd like to help a friend with wrong views, you might need to listen to his views first and even agree with him here or there, and then, when the time comes, provide the right view at the right time and gradually guide him.

Certainly, if you don't think you have the capacity, then you shouldn't comply with them. Otherwise, you might find their views appeal to you, and instead of converting their views, you adopt them. Then doesn't it become "following the bad example of others" instead of "serving others so as to suit their needs"?

I'm working in the media. These days some people wear the robes of a guru, but I've witnessed their selfish and inappropriate behavior. What should I do? Should I turn a blind eye to it or alert other people?

It depends. If they could harm a wide range of people, it's wise to alert the public. However, at the same time, avoid bringing negative attention to Buddhism.

These days, many Tibetan Buddhist lamas have been teaching in Chinese areas, teaching them to take refuge, generate bodhichitta, and practice virtue. As a result, a great number of people have taken refuge, learned the Dharma, and been taken care of by their teachers. This is great.

Meanwhile, some people have been here for their own interest. Lacking Buddhist education, some unsophisticated people in Chinese areas impetuously rely on and make offerings to lamas whom they've never met before, let alone examined. After some problems come up, they lose faith, hold wrong views, and even file lawsuits. Just as different commercial products, genuine or fake, emerge on the market, scenarios like this do happen.

Should we speak out after witnessing such things? It depends on whether we're able to stop it, and whether the effect is positive if we do.

If you have the capacity and are sure the effect will be positive, then stop them. However, after examining the situation, if you find it won't help them, you can't change them, and it will bring harm to Buddhism, then it might be good to say nothing.

Why? Once you report it, as we all know, people these days do blame the person who has the issue, and they would be more likely to say "Tibetan Buddhism is such and such," and "Chinese Buddhism is such as such." Although this person doesn't represent any school or tradition, once the scandal is out, it harms the image of Buddhism as a whole, not to mention the virtuous roots of many people.

Moreover, we already have plenty of negative reports on Buddhism in the media. Afraid of protest, journalists avoid producing negative reports about other religions. However, since they're not afraid of Buddhism, they constantly report, "Today, the monk so and so has done such and such," and "Today, such and such happened at a Buddhist monastery." No matter what they say, we Buddhists seem too "compassionate" to care. As a result, Buddhism has often faced discrimination.

Therefore, I believe we need more laws that could protect Buddhism and positive reports that could help society widely acknowledge Buddhism.

One of my friends just lost her mother and was overcome with grief. I recommended your book Tales for Transforming Adversity *to her. After reading it, she really wanted to see you. She would've loved to have attended your talk today, but due to the regulations of the China Culture College, she couldn't, so she's extremely sad. I'm unhappy too, so I just want to complain about this, nothing else.*

It's necessary to respect the regulations of the Culture College. However, since your friend is in agony, I can meet her tonight or tomorrow morning if she would like to see me. People grieve the most when relatives pass away, and they need others' support. If you haven't yet experienced it, you may not understand, and you may ask, "Why are you crying your heart out?" "Why are you so sorrowful?" But for those who are in that scenario, it's so hard to get over it.

In the past, I was asked to chant prayers for recently deceased people in our Buddhist institute, but I seldom went. However, after my father passed away, I also went to request prayers from some lamas and tulkus. Some accepted, some turned me down. Although I knew they had a busy schedule, I felt depressed and thought, "My father died! Why can't you accept my request for chanting prayers?"

I've experienced it, so I understand her pain. Empathy could be a kind of practice.

Meditation is practiced quietly in general, but can I practice it while active? For instance, can I chant om mani padme hum *every time I hit a ball? If this is allowed, it would be easier to integrate practice into my life.*

It depends on how developed your practice is. Generally, beginners should practice while sitting still. Whether chanting or performing visualization practices, it will be easy to practice with a peaceful body and mind.

After reaching some level of realization, it doesn't matter if you encounter some distractions. In secret Mantrayana, sometimes, with some degree of realization, you're asked to run, sing, and do other such things as part of your practice. You could still be focused and reach higher states of realization through this kind of practice.

Each individual has different faculties. If you can chant *om mani padme hum* while playing basketball, that's great. But if you end up forgetting to chant and only playing, then it's better to devote some time to practice while sitting still.

You said we should count the mantras we recite, but I always lose track on how many I've recited. Is this okay?
It's better to count them. If you just recite without counting, it's not reliable. You think you've done a lot, but you may have just recited the mantra ten times. If you count each one and have a clear idea of your accumulations, it will motivate your practice.

Sometimes when I study the Dharma in my workplace, many colleagues are curious and want to talk about Buddhism with me. They read Buddhist books by themselves and express their personal views on Buddhism. In many cases, I can easily tell they misunderstand Buddhism and sometimes even slander the Dharma. Afraid of upsetting them, I don't feel that it's appropriate to refute them directly. How should I guide them skillfully?
In order to guide others, we need to study well the doctrines and receive a comprehensive education in Buddhism.

I was told that on one occasion, a great master gave a lecture on Sutrayana and Mantrayana here. Someone asked the person sitting next to him, "What is Sutrayana and Mantrayana?" That person answered, "Sutrayana is Sutrayana, Mantrayana is Mantrayana."

I'm sure many people don't know the difference and can't give a good answer to this. In order to systematically study the Dharma, Buddhists should have a qualified teacher to guide them. This is different from having never studied or read books on one's own.

By reading alone, you might acquire some knowledge, but it's difficult to understand the actual meaning. Without understanding the actual meaning, as you mentioned, they may slander the Dharma. It would be nice if you could suggest that they study the Dharma under the guidance of a qualified teacher.

Without a lineage, even Master Yongjia Xuanjue couldn't be acknowledged, let alone ordinary people. He told Chan Master Xuan Ce that he had realized the heart essence of the Buddha while reading the *Vimalakirti Sutra*. Master Xuan Ce said, "Those who are enlightened without a teacher are called natural heretics."

He asked Xuan Ce to acknowledge his enlightenment. Xuan Ce said, "My realization isn't adequate. You should go look for the Sixth Patriarch in Cao Xi." Master Yongjia presented himself to the Sixth Patriarch, Huineng, who confirmed his enlightenment.

Seeing people study the Dharma by themselves, we should inspire them to receive some authentic Buddhist education based on their virtuous roots. When we guide them, we should be skillful. There's no need to identify some "misdeed" to them. Otherwise, they would be annoyed.

However, when using reasoning, you must be able to refute their view.

There's no need to be too modest. If someone believes he is right, without reservation, you can use Buddhist theories to show him what's right and what's wrong. Otherwise, he might think that even a trained Buddhist can't debate with him and that his view is correct and should be spread everywhere. That would be bad for him.

We must study well first. Then, with skillful means, we can easily refute their statements out of context.

How does one transform afflictive emotions on the path?
The *Sutra of the Sixth Patriarch* states, "Afflictive emotions are enlightenment." To understand the meaning of this remark and apply it to your practice is to transform afflictive emotions on the path.

For instance, when feelings of desire or hatred arise in you, you can examine their whereabouts: Where do they come from? Where do they reside? Where do they go? In this way, you'll find that afflictive emotions don't exist.

Afflictive emotions aren't the only things that don't exist; even the person who bears them and the objects that enkindle them don't exist. If I nourish hatred toward this person, does the essence of "I" exist? Does the essence of "this person" exist? Does the essence of "hatred" exist? If you search thoroughly and repeatedly, you'll reach the conclusion that none of them exist: "I" is unfindable, "enemy" is unfindable, and "hatred" is unfindable. They can't be found either inside or outside. Therefore, we say "unfindable."

Everything is empty by nature; their appearance is just the display of wisdom.

While examining and sincerely realizing this point, you're in the process of transforming afflictive emotions on the path, because you've already understood their essence is emptiness. If this is the case, afflictive emotions won't remain.

Certainly, this requires practice. It won't work if you just rely on book learning or merely say words aloud. Imagine that an enemy is coming. Would it work if you just cried out "the enemy doesn't exist, the enemy doesn't exist" and ran away? Similarly, when an afflictive emotion arises, would it work if you cried out "this afflictive emotion doesn't exist, it doesn't exist" while it escalates?

Therefore, realize the nature of afflictive emotions by all means! Once realized, they can't do any harm.

Many people in my workplace have studied the Dharma, and every day I hear them say, "My lama is so and so. Who's your lama?" I haven't yet taken refuge, but I've found your lectures are quite interesting, so I like to listen to them. You mentioned that in order to examine a lama properly, one should spend five or six years doing so. This fits my style. Besides, you're not like people who put themselves on the air. Sorry for saying that. So, my question is this: Is taking refuge required for everyone studying the Dharma?

Actually, expressing one's own thinking frankly when exchanging ideas is something I admire. You're very cautious about taking refuge, which I think is much wiser than taking refuge after hearing only a name without further examination.

It's okay if you don't feel ready to take refuge in the beginning. Some people mistakenly think that the object of taking refuge is the person, so after taking refuge, they treat their lama as their personal property: "He's my lama, not yours."

I heard about a lama who has two groups of disciples in the same city. Once, as soon as he walked out of the airport, the two groups of people fought to snatch him. One group grabbed his body and the other group his robes. It ended very poorly.

This isn't a problem in Christianity. They have faith in the same God. Their priests wouldn't say, "This is my disciple" and the disciples wouldn't say, "This is my priest." So, they're in harmony. In fact, this is also the case for us who take refuge in the same Three Jewels. Therefore, every time I say, "On behalf of the Three Jewels, the Buddha, the Dharma, and the Sangha, I bestow refuge to you," you're taking refuge in the Three Jewels, not me.

Why do I say it this way? On one hand, if I make any mistake, I won't dishonor other people. On the other hand, I do it to discourage people from claiming "mine" and "yours" with attachment. We're all Buddhist followers, disciples of the Buddha, so we should be in harmony.

Surely, the intentions and faculties of each individual are different. Not all people have to follow the same path we've chosen; they have the freedom to choose their own. Our beliefs may be completely different, but this doesn't hinder our common goal. Therefore, taking refuge depends on causes and conditions. When causes and conditions ripen, one naturally takes refuge just as a fully ripened fruit falls to the ground.

However, since this human body is very difficult to obtain, when causes and conditions ripen, make sure you don't miss it. You also need to know that with or without taking refuge, the merit and willpower of a person make a great difference.

I don't know why, but every time I read the Diamond Sutra, *I'm drowsy. What is the reason?*

Could it be that the blessings of this sutra calm your mind? I should give this a try the next time I can't fall asleep.

In regard to relying on gurus, you suggested examining them for five or six years. I believe this is appropriate and the safest way. However, if everyone spends such a long time examining a teacher, will it hinder the progress of Buddhism? Are there any exceptions?

Just as nine-year compulsory education doesn't prevent the development of China but instead facilitates its progress, to examine a guru for five or six years shouldn't hinder the progress of Buddhism. It's necessary to engage in long-term preparation for important things.

In fact, to examine a guru, sometimes it requires even more time. According to Tsongkhapa's commentary on the *Fifty Verses of Guru Devotion*, one should examine a potential guru for twelve years.

There are also exceptions. For some well-acknowledged great masters, you can rely on them without examination. In the past, Khenpo Deba told me, "Theoretically, it's right to examine a guru for a long time, but for a great practitioner like Kyabjé Jigme Phuntsok Rinpoché, who's acknowledged worldwide for his immense contribution to spreading the Dharma and benefiting sentient beings, you don't have the ability to examine him, and there's no need to examine him. You can rely on him right away."

After hearing this, I immediately went to rely on him in Larung Gar.

In the doctrines of the Great Perfection, there are three concepts: the essence is emptiness, the nature is luminous, and great compassion is pervasive. However, contemporary Humanistic Buddhism advocates unconditional loving-kindness and compassion concerned with all, while the Chan school only emphasizes emptiness. Does this mean that only the doctrine of the Great Perfection has integrated the three aspects together?

It's in order to describe the different facets of pure awareness or *rigpa* that Nyingmapas say, "The essence is emptiness, the nature is luminous, and great compassion is pervasive." So, these three are originally one.

Therefore, this isn't the ultimate integration of the views of various schools or traditions, but rather the attributes of three facets spontaneously present when one recognizes the nature of mind. "The essence is emptiness" is the dharmakaya; "the nature is luminous" is the sambhogakaya; and "great compassion is pervasive" is the nirmanakaya emanated variously among sentient beings.

I often arrange for Dharma brothers to chant prayers for the dying or the recently deceased. However, some individuals have some misgivings: they're afraid that the deceased will hurt them and bring unwholesome effects on them and their family. My question is, Are these misgivings necessary?

If the deceased died naturally from disease or old age, they won't harm you. According to some folklore in Tibet, if the deceased died unexpectedly due to violence, they might attempt to do something. However, this can be avoided by chanting prayers.

Chanting prayers for the dying or the recently deceased requires great aspiration, so the merit generated is also great.

Although there are various kinds of folklore about this, it's unnecessary to have those misgivings because the names and mantras of buddhas and bodhisattvas are completely capable of protecting you and preventing them from harming you. Besides, with pure intention, your chanting has inconceivable benefit for the deceased.

Previously, for an entire year, I managed to get up at five o'clock in the morning to study and do my morning chanting. Afterward, I made an aspiration to take the eight Mahayana precepts for forty-nine days, and I hoped to get up a bit earlier to have more time to study. Who would've thought that after thirty days, I still can't get up until five o'clock. It seems I can't get up now.

Haven't you already gotten up today??

It's better to plan one's Dharma practice according to one's health. This requires adjustment in the long run. It's inappropriate to have only occasional diligence.

In order to make more time for Dharma practice, the first step is to cut your sleep time. Oversleeping is just a habitual tendency, so it can be reduced little by little. The second thing is to reduce distraction. Many people complain about having no time for Dharma practice, but in fact, instead of no time, their time is spent on various distractions.

I'm a volunteer working at the Kindness & Wisdom Foundation. During my internship, I had the opportunity to spend time with old people and found that they're so lonely and helpless. At the same time, I noticed that some volunteers aren't so into this work because they think it's mundane and irrelevant to their supramundane pursuits. Some are unwilling to follow the management's rules. However, I believe that engaging in charity can cultivate bodhichitta. How can we cultivate our mind through charitable activities?

It hasn't been very long since I began engaging in charity, but it was a letter from a girl that first inspired me to act.

At that time, she was about to drop out of middle school because her family was too poor, so she wrote me a letter and tried to deliver it to me. However, I was in the Chinese area at that time, and when I returned to our institute, I didn't see her letter. Still hoping to continue her education, she wrote me another letter and this time I got it.

In her letter, she wrote, "I've been wishing to live a life developing my own intelligence, but my family is too poor to support me in my education. I heard you're a khenpo. I don't know if you could possibly help me." At the end of the letter, she left her neighbor's landline phone number.

Previously, I had never provided financial support to needy students. After reading her letter, I tried to contact her and finally found her after lots of twists. I started to support her. Now she has already graduated and become a doctor in Palyul County in Garze Tibetan Autonomous Prefecture. She's very grateful for the support I provided.

This event has changed many of my ideas about generosity. In the past, I thought it's enough to take good care of my own practice and virtuous actions. It was she who inspired me to start engaging in charitable work. I told her the other day, "It was your letter that inspired me to support people and change their fate."

Are these efforts considered mundane? Yes. When you go to see elders and provide care to them, this is also mundane. But is it necessary for a person pursuing supramundane Dharma to engage in them? Yes, it's necessary.

Although your practice involves the great compassion of emptiness, you can't apply it in places other than these. When you actually engage in such activities, you may find your compassion is far from enough, but when you occasionally succeed, your practice will become even more inspired. Therefore, mundane and supramundane practices aren't contradictory. We're not going to quit practicing Dharma in order to engage in these activities every day.

Do charitable activities require management?

I believe that management according to regulations and laws is necessary. Although we're Buddhists and practice virtue, it still won't work without good management. When our guru Jigme Phuntsok Rinpoché was in this world, he also had various management rules in regard to khenpos, tulkus, and all other ordinary monastics in our institute. So, appropriate management is quite important.

Without management, even practicing virtue can't be entirely satisfactory. People may send gifts to children on Children's Day or June 1 and go to take care of elders on Elder's Day or the day of the Double Ninth Festival. But how about afterward? Nobody follows up. Practicing virtue also requires management to ensure that our efforts to help others steadily continue with moderate exertion.

I've been saying "Charity comes from the heart." Once the wish to practice virtue arises in you, you'll naturally want to devote time to charity. Everyone has the ability to practice virtue, and people who need help are everywhere. But without an altruistic heart, even when brushing past a great number of people, you won't notice any of the miserable people or their suffering. If even Buddhists act like this, who else will care for them?

We often think of ourselves as Mahayana bodhisattvas, but whether we are or not depends on how we act rather than what we say. Christianity doesn't have extensive doctrines like Buddhism, but their followers actually devote themselves to their beliefs and to sentient beings, which is more convincing than the practices we perform for the sake of ourselves. It also reflects a stronger power of virtue.

Just now somebody said that when he visited Bodhgaya, he made an aspiration to do virtuous deeds. This is great. Whether it's helping ailing people or old people, do what you can. If you only have the ability to help five people, take good care of the five people, and spend fifty years making it perfect. If you can help ten people, help ten. If you don't start helping others and only live for your own sake, you'll regret that your life has passed by so meaninglessly.

In fact, our wealth and social status are from the merit we've accumulated over many lifetimes and our efforts to help others. Therefore, according to the law of karmic cause and effect, we have no excuse to enjoy life by ourselves while making no contribution to society.

When I was cycling in the Tibetan area, I passed a mountain called Mount Kailash. Local people told me that according to Hinduism and Tibetan Buddhism, it's a sacred mountain and circumambulating it once can purify the misdeeds of an entire lifetime. So, I did two circumambulations. Is this a reliable practice?

Circumambulating sacred mountains generates tremendous merit. This is true of Mount Kailash in particular. I myself have been longing to go on a pilgrimage to it. In the biographies of many great lamas, they treat circumambulating Mount Kailash, Mount Tsari, and Haixin Mountain in Qinghai Lake as part of their spiritual practice. So, these places are of great power of blessing.

In regard to what the local people said, if it's not provisional and indeed fact, then as long as you have a pure heart with powers like those of the great masters, then your misdeeds can be purified. Even if you can't do it perfectly due to your karma and effort in practice, there's no doubt that a considerable portion of your misdeeds can be purified.

I have two kids, one eight, one two. Could you please give me some advice and warnings regarding childhood education?
It's universally accepted that prenatal influences, education at home, education in school, and societal education are indispensable for raising a child appropriately. Among them, some people believe the influence of parents is very important.

Education is for cultivating good character among children. However, after traditional culture was devastated in the Chinese areas, people began neglecting the importance of educating children on how to relate to people, how to behave nicely, and how to be a good person. Therefore, I suggest that parents should give children the opportunity to study the *Standards for Being a Good Pupil and Child* as well as the *Three Character Classic* and even the *Difference of Karmic Effect Sutra* in Buddhism. In this way, they can develop notions of morality and cause and effect from childhood onward.

I really wish schools would provide this kind of education. Teachers who are aware of its importance could tell children stories, ancient or contemporary, on being dutiful to parents and being kind to others. This can be quite edificatory for their little hearts. Otherwise, if we only focus on their performance grades and exam scores, their future won't be extraordinarily bright.

These days there are many talented people, but not many who are *really* talented. When they're recruited with their bachelor's degree, master's degree, or even PhD degree, their diplomas look good, but once they actually start working, they don't even have the basic ability to get along with other people. This isn't a small issue. They themselves are also in distress. They wonder, "I've been in school all these years and have equipped myself with great knowledge. Why can't I understand these people? Why am I frustrated by society?"

Therefore, it's important to consider what you'll teach your children. If Confucianism and Buddhism could be spread in the home and in schools, children could develop a kind disposition from an early age. Then we wouldn't have to worry so much.

Some of Tsangyang Gyatso's poems discuss romantic affection.[18] *I can't understand them. Could you please explain them?*
With genuine bodhichitta, one can liberate sentient beings based on present conditions, just as buddhas and bodhisattvas can emanate in a variety of embodiments according to what will benefit a particular group of beings. Their love isn't stained with the afflictive emotions of possessing someone, and at the same time, their love doesn't include attachment. As it's said, "Just like sun and moon that course unhindered through the sky." It's their skillful means that benefit others.

However, we ordinary beings don't have the realization of noble beings. Our love focuses on the possession of others and selfishness, so we shouldn't emulate noble beings in this way.

Since you've promoted having a loving heart in action, I've been
active in animal protection and have saved many stray animals.
In this process, I've found many people are indifferent to animals
and even harm them. Would you please give some instructions
and suggestions?

We protect animals because they feel the same things we do: suffering and happiness, love and hatred.

Not long ago, there was this news story: On someone's balcony in Chongqing, there was a female cat who gave birth to five kittens. Every day, she went out for food and came back to feed her babies. After a couple of weeks, a vicious idea came to the owner, who decided to push the kittens off the balcony, killing all of them. After returning, the mother cat found her babies' bodies. Very strangely, she picked them up and placed them one after another in front of the owner's door. Then she left. About a month later, the owner was diagnosed with skin cancer.

This is a real story. Some people believe it was the mother cat's revenge, and that the person who killed her babies deserved this consequence.

If we say this demonstrates the law of karmic cause and effect, many people wouldn't understand what we mean. So, let's put aside this concept and just think of the feelings experienced by the cat. Was she distressed? Did she feel hatred? Countless people believe that it doesn't matter if we harm or kill animals and that it's right and proper to eat them. However, animals also have feelings. If you take this into consideration, you might be able to understand why we should have compassion for them.

Many people say the merit generated by saving people is immense, but this is also true for saving animals. If you can help stray animals, protect them, and feed them, it's a very meaningful virtuous deed. The more you can engage in it the better.

If you spend a long time on one project, you'll gain abilities that allow you to do it well in different contexts. With great effort, you'll see the actual effect after eight or ten years or even several decades. Otherwise, if you're enthusiastic about one thing today but switch to another thing tomorrow, you'll end up getting nowhere in the end.

I really rejoice in your efforts to help animals. In the West, the concept of protecting animals is rather mature. Last year in France and Spain, naked protesters demonstrated against animal maltreatment.

Personally, I believe this upholds equality. Like human beings, animals also have feelings. Western people are aware of this, but some of us haven't yet understood it.

I have a Tibetan mastiff and treat him like my son. Not long ago, he jumped from the fourth floor, but he eventually recovered. However, now he has started to harm himself and gnawed his legs to the bone. Doctors and friends all suggested euthanasia, but I can't make a decision. Please tell me, should I let him live or let him go?

Let him live. It would be a great fault to take his life.

My friend is pregnant, but her doctor found the baby has defects and suggested that she abort it. My friend is a devout Buddhist and knows that abortion is a serious misdeed just like taking one's life. What should she do?

Buddhism believes that every life has value—not just the lives of human beings, but each and every sentient being.

None of us has the right to say, "Such and such a life can be taken." To suggest abortion is an immense misdeed.

At a business dinner, most people don't believe in Buddhism and want to eat meat and even freshly killed fish and lobsters. I've tried many times, but I've only dissuaded a few of them. How can we avoid killing for the dinner table?

There's no easy solution for this. The majority of people are non-Buddhists, and the temptation of meat is strong, so it's unrealistic to stop them from killing or consuming meat. The Sixth Patriarch had to eat the veggies beside the meat when he lived with hunters. If you have no other choice, you might have to do the same.

However, it's hard to say after eating veggies beside meat whether or not you might begin eating meat beside veggies as time goes by. I understand your difficulty. You want to avoid meat as a good Buddhist on one hand, but you have to comply with partners at work on the other. Even if this is the case, I still suggest that you try to be vegetarian, which is a very good tradition.

In accordance with the doctrines of Mahayana Buddhism, this tradition started at the time of Emperor Wu of Liang and is a direct attempt to protect the lives of others. Otherwise, if one hundred people have dinner together and they're all meat-eaters, it's not enough to kill one pig. Imagine if we have to eat meat for each meal. How many lives have to be taken? I read a book saying, "To eat meat is to eat lives." This isn't alarmist talk.

Our way of thinking can be altered. In Tibetan Buddhism, eating meat has been a tradition for a long time due to the poor farming conditions in Tibet. However, in recent years, many great masters in Tibet have promoted a vegetarian diet as an example that we should follow from the traditions of Chinese Buddhism. In our Buddhist institute, when we have Dharma gatherings, thousands of people all eat vegetarian meals together and more and more people become vegetarian. This is unprecedented.

If we say in the Buddhist community that adopting a vegetarian diet is done out of compassion, it's easy to promote. However, in order to convince people with a non-Buddhist background to give up eating meat, we can also advise them from the perspective of better health and nutrition. Multiple medical studies have reported that the human digestive system is unsuitable for consuming meat, and we can get enough nutrition eating only vegetarian food.

I often joke that "Yaks only eat grass, but they're very strong." And many vegetarians' great health also demonstrates that a vegetarian diet is healthy.

Not being able to adopt a vegetarian diet is mainly due to having a strong habitual tendency toward eating meat. Many people can't skip meat even for one meal. When I discussed building a school in my hometown with local government officials, we had meetings for a couple of days. At first, they wanted to show respect and only had vegetarian meals with me, but finally they couldn't tolerate it, and one of them said, "I've had vegetarian meals for three days in a row, and I even had diarrhea today. Your Buddhist life is a great hardship!" I laughed, saying, "Really. Lots of Buddhists in Chinese areas eat no meat every day for years and they're very healthy. Don't relate things improperly."

In Buddhism, it says, "All the Dharma taught by the Buddha was for liberating minds. Since there's no mind at all, what is the use of all the Dharma?" Does this mean there's no need to use the Dharma in the end?

Right. This is explained from its essence. Since mind doesn't exist, there's no need to use the Dharma, but at the level of appearance, we still have to use the Dharma.

When can we stop using the Dharma?

When we reach genuine enlightenment.

After the mind of renunciation arises, how do we deal with our responsibilities to our children and parents?

Many people believe that having a strong mind of renunciation involves not caring for family members. This is actually wrong. *The Three Principles of the Path* states that by meditating on the difficulty of obtaining a human body and the impermanence of life, we can be weary of the present life; by meditating on the defects of cyclic existence and the infallible law of karmic cause and effect, we can give up attachment to future lives. This is the genuine mind of renunciation.

With such a mind of renunciation, one is neither attached to wealth and honor nor gives thought to personal gains and losses. One is just happy to lead a simple life. One should also comply with worldly customs and conventions and be responsible for one's duties. Moreover, one should generate bodhichitta and respect and comply with parents, children, and even all living beings just as one treats a bodhisattva. So, renunciation isn't indifference, but rather a form of wisdom that favors family harmony.

After generating bodhichitta, how can we strengthen our will-power and ability?

Through great aspiration and great strength. The bodhisat-tva Nagarjuna said that one who has genuine bodhichitta is a real Mahayana practitioner, even when he doesn't engage in actual altruistic action.

Bodhichitta is the root of Mahayana Buddhism. Weak willpower results mainly from the limitations of selfish thinking. Your willpower can become stronger when you understand more about the merit of altruism and the harm of selfishness. Once your willpower is strong, your ability is strong.

I have the feeling that whether it's charitable work or running a school, once I've made a great aspiration, all sorts of supportive resources and causes and conditions are present. If I don't make this kind of aspiration, I'll only hear complaints about how it's not feasible, doesn't work, and can't be done.

After a breakup, a young man became depressed and wanted to commit suicide. Does this result from causes and conditions from previous lives?

Some might trace this back to previous lives, but not 100 percent. Some things are consequences of the causes and conditions of the present life. Nevertheless, there's no need to commit suicide after a breakup. I often say that there's not just one path in life. If this one really can't work out, give the one over there a try.

In the *White Lotus: Buddha Shakyamuni's Great Biography*, there's a story about how an infatuated woman became insane after her husband's death. Carrying his corpse on her back, she wandered around the charnel ground until the corpse became a skeleton. At that time, the Buddha was born as a physician named Gesharpa. After he met this poor woman, great compassion arose in him. He found a female skeleton, carried it on his back, and went before her.

After spending some time with her, he waited for her to fall asleep. He then tied the two skeletons together and threw them into a nearby river. He cried out loudly to wake her up and shouted, "Your husband enticed my wife away!" Seeing this, the woman was furious. After being comforted for a while, she became sane again.

Essentially, people's affections are just a transient connection. Often when we look back after ten or twenty years, the earlier strong attachment seems ridiculous.

My greatest wish is to build a school in Sichuan, Tibet, Yunnan, or Guizhou. However, I'm not sure if the students will take refuge in Buddhism when they grow up. Some Dharma friends suggested that I make offerings to lamas or build monasteries, because only these projects spread the Dharma and benefit sentient beings. Where should I put my effort?

It's better to make a decision about building a school or monastery by yourself. If you decide to build a school, it's not important whether the students become Buddhists or not. What's important is that after receiving a good education, they have a bright future and happy life. This is my purpose for running schools.

However, it's not easy to run a school. Initially, you need to build it, then you have to manage and maintain it. Lots of effort is required across different domains. You'll also have to face all of these issues if you choose to build a monastery, but the key will be whether it will help spread the Dharma and benefit sentient beings.

It's easy to talk about impermanence, but it's hard to face it when it really happens. Especially when parents or children suddenly pass away, you just feel completely unprepared. I wish you could give us some instructions on this.

Indeed. We know that impermanence is imminent for ourselves and those around us; it's inevitable. But once it comes, it's still so hard to face. Nevertheless, it's good to remain mindful of impermanence at every moment, whether you're a practitioner or not. Steve Jobs, for example, used to ask himself every morning if this was his last day.

Personally, I dare not brag about other practices, but I do practice impermanence each and every day. Every time I read about the passing of great masters and kings from ancient times, I meditate on impermanence. When it happens around me, whether it's children seeing the death of their parents or parents seeing the death of their children, I also meditate on impermanence.

In his *Recollections of Shadows and Dust,* Master Tanxu explains that a family was joyfully preparing for a wedding, but one person died, so the wedding turned into a funeral.[19] Not long ago, one of my classmates suddenly passed away. He was in great shape, but when it was time, it was time— nobody could do anything. Over the past two days, we've gathered here, but afterward, some of us may see each other again while others may never see each other. These are all impermanent.

Life is a textbook on impermanence, and each and every person plays a role in it. As long as we remind ourselves about impermanence and meditate on it constantly, we'll naturally gain the strength and power to face it. This can't be achieved through book learning.

This is why great masters of the past have said, "If you choose to focus on only one practice, meditate on impermanence." Meditate on impermanence, because initially, it can be a major cause leading you to Buddhism; in the middle, it can be the condition urging you to practice diligently; and finally, it can be the companion that helps you realize the equality of all phenomena.

Q&A session at China Culture College
December 23, 2012

AFTERWORD

NOWADAYS, MANY PEOPLE keep their eyes glued to their cell-phones, looking at them constantly while walking, eating, or exercising. Their "busyness" is nothing more than this.

Such busyness robs them of their freedom. A famous person once said, "Where does freedom come from? It comes from self-confidence. Self-confidence, in turn, comes from self-discipline, which is the ability to strictly manage one's time."

This is very well said. Learn to use your time effectively and meaningfully, and examine your mind once in a while. Stop being so "busy" all day long.

Let me share one of my favorite poems with you. Hopefully, it will help you understand busyness in a different way.

> With bustle and hustle, we chase things while in pain.
> Being cold and hot, we then go through spring and fall.
> From dawn till dusk, we take care of our family.
> In confusion and muddle, we go gray.
> Disputes and conflicts, when will you end?
> Anger and annoyance, when will you rest?
> Clearly and obviously, the path is laid out.
> The teachings are countless—you just refuse to follow them.[20]

Sodargye
January 24, 2015

NOTES

1. Liu Zhen (460–501) was a painter and writer.

2. The real name of Emperor Po Yang (550–89) was Chen Boshan.

3. Lu Ban, or Gongshu Yizhi, was a Zhou-dynasty-era carpenter and inventor revered in Chinese folklore as the patron of builders and contractors.

4. Illicit cooking oil that has been recycled from waste oil collected from sources such as restaurant fryers, grease traps, slaughterhouse waste, and sewage from sewer drains.

5. *Dream of Nanke* and *A Golden Millet Dream* refer to Chinese stories in which most of the plot takes place inside a dream.

6. Banesh Hoffmann, Helen Dukas, and Albert Einstein. *Albert Einstein, The Human Side: Glimpses from His Archives* (Princeton, NJ: Princeton University Press, 2013).

7. Some people may argue, "Plants are also a form of life. If Buddhism advocates not killing animals, they should also restrain from killing plants." In fact, animals and plants are very different. Although both of them have life, plants are not composed of the five aggregates.

8. The city where Guangxi Normal University is located.

9. Lu Xun was the pen name of Zhou Shuren (1881–1936), one of the foremost modern Chinese writers.

10. The *Four Lessons of Liao Fan* is book written in the Ming Dynasty by Yuan Liao Fan as a set of lessons for his son on how to change one's fate through acts of kindness and humility. It's considered an important text in Confucianism and Chinese Buddhism.

11. Langdarma was a Tibetan emperor who reigned from approximately 838 to 841 CE. Said to be a practitioner of Bön, he repressed Buddhist practice in Tibet.

12. Zhuangzi, also known as Chuang Tzu, was a Chinese philosopher who lived around the fourth century BCE and was the author of an influential Daoist text of the same name.

13. The *Standards for Being a Good Pupil and Child (Di Zi Gui)* and the *Three Character Classic (San Zi Jing)* are classic Chinese texts that distill Confucianism in a manner suitable for children.

14. Nan Huaijin (1918–2012) was a master of Chinese Buddhism and philosophy who was considered to be the major force in the revival of Chinese Buddhism. Many of his books have been translated into English, including *Diamond Sutra Explained*.

15. The *Book of Rites* is a core Confucian text; it outlines the social and ceremonial norms of the Zhou dynasty as they were understood in the Warring States and the early Han periods.

16. Hanshan ("Cold Mountain") and Shide were Tang-dynasty-era poets, considered by the Chinese Buddhist tradition to be emanations of the bodhisattvas Manjushri and Samantabhadra, respectively.

17. Ji Gong (1130–1209), born Li Xiuyuan, was a Chan monk and Chinese folk hero known for championing the poor and disregarding monastic rules and for his carefree nature.

18. Tsangyang Gyatso (1683–1706) was the sixth Dalai Lama. His poems, which often deal with love, are popular across Tibet and China.

19. Master Tanxu (1875–1963), born as Wang Futing, was a monk and lineage holder of the Tiantai school. He's renowned for building temples and reinvigorating Buddhist practice in northern China. *Recollections of Shadows and Dust* is his autobiography.

20. This was composed by Luodian during the Ming Dynasty.

About the Author

 KHENPO SODARGYE WAS born in Tibet in 1962 in what is today the Sichuan Province of China. He spent his early years herding yaks, and after attending Garzé Normal School entered Larung Gar Buddhist Institute in Sêrtar, becoming a monk in 1985 under the great Jigme Phuntsok Rinpoché. Khenpo served Rinpoché as his personal and teaching interpreter on overseas tours in Asia, Europe, and North America as well as at Larung Gar. Khenpo has taught and translated the Dharma for over thirty years and has lectured on Buddhism and social issues in over a hundred universities around the world. He is one of the leading scholars at Larung Gar and has popularized Tibetan Buddhism among Han Chinese students with numerous bestselling books.

WHAT TO READ NEXT
FROM WISDOM PUBLICATIONS

TALES FOR TRANSFORMING ADVERSITY
A Buddhist Lama's Advice for Life's Ups and Downs
Khenpo Sodargye

"I'd like to think that *Tales for Transforming Adversity* may cause some people to rethink their life. It is not a panacea for every spiritual ill, but I hope that it may bring peace and joy to some people's minds in this turbulent age."
—Khenpo Sodargye

ALWAYS REMEMBERING
Heartfelt Advice for Your Entire Life
Jigme Phuntsok and Khenpo Sodargye

"*Always Remembering* offers an illuminating glimpse of the wisdom of Jigme Phuntsok Rinpoché grounded in the nomadic grasslands of eastern Tibet, reminding us of impermanence with poetic elegance, inspiring us to diligently seek out spiritual instruction, and advising us how to conduct ourselves virtuously in daily life."
—Sarah Jacoby, Northwestern University

The Path
A Guide to Happiness
Khenpo Sherab Zangpo

Khenpo Sherab Zangpo draws on the Tibetan Buddhist tradition and his own fascinating life story to describe a way forward for contemporary practitioners, offering clear guidance on daily practice, finding the right teacher, and cultivating a wiser and more compassionate attitude toward others and ourselves.

Vajrasattva Meditation
An Illustrated Guide
Khenpo Yeshe Phunstok

Combining prayers, visualizations, mantras, and multiple styles of meditation, the practice of Vajrasattva meditation is an entryway into the performance of the complex tantric sadhana rituals that are central to Tibetan Buddhism. Accompanied by more than forty color illustrations, this friendly volume is the perfect practical guide for both beginners and experienced practitioners.

Living and Dying with Confidence
A Day-by-Day Guide
Anyen Rinpoche

"Anyen Rinpoche has skillfully woven the Dharma teachings into these everyday contemplations on death, which will be very beneficial, especially for those in denial or dealing with loss. This is a handbook of daily instruction to prepare us all for our inevitable separations, losses, and death and at the same time nurture the

appreciation that all these situations are essential ingredients on the spiritual path."
—Tenzin Palmo, founder of Dongyu Gatsal Ling Nunnery

NOT ONE SINGLE THING
A Commentary on the Platform Sūtra
Shodo Harada

"These teachings are deep . . . the light of this genuine Zen master's profound clarity shines through!"
—Ven. Mitra Bishop, abbot, Mountain Gate, and spiritual director, Hidden Valley Zen Center

About Wisdom Publications

Wisdom Publications is the leading publisher of classic and contemporary Buddhist books and practical works on mindfulness. To learn more about us or to explore our other books, please visit our website at wisdomexperience.org or contact us at the address below.

Wisdom Publications
199 Elm Street
Somerville, MA 02144 USA

We are a 501(c)(3) organization, and donations in support of our mission are tax deductible.

Wisdom Publications is affiliated with the Foundation for the Preservation of the Mahayana Tradition (FPMT).